"I am very grateful for this second edition ... *Freaking Out*. A really good book is now ... Biblically faithful and extremely practical, it will equip anyone who has himself been transformed by the gospel to share that same life-changing message with confidence and competence. Read it and then go tell someone about Jesus."

—**Daniel L. Akin**, president, Southeastern
Baptist Theological Seminary

"Hildreth and McKinion offer readers a theologically sound, yet practical and engaging call to a lifestyle of evangelism. They remind us all that evangelism for Christians is natural, normal, relational, and that we all have a compelling story of redemption to share. Having known both of these men for more than a decade, I am so excited for this book to get into the hands of Christians in the workplace, on the mission field, and in the pews."

—**Paul M. Akin**, dean, Billy Graham School of Missions,
Evangelism and Ministry and assistant professor of Christian
missions, The Southern Baptist Theological Seminary

"As human beings we regularly take simple concepts and make them overly complex. That tendency often happens with the subject of evangelism. I am delighted to recommend this helpful resource by Scott Hildreth and Steve McKinion. As professors, they keep this book biblically and theologically sound; as practitioners, they remind us of the simplicity of evangelism. Read this book and be encouraged as you seek to bear witness for Christ!"

—**Timothy K. Beougher**, associate dean, Billy Graham
School of Missions, Evangelism and Ministry and Billy
Graham Professor of Evangelism and Church Growth,
The Southern Baptist Theological Seminary

"There's a reason this title resonates with today's believers. We want to share Jesus in a winsome way, but don't quite know how. *Sharing Jesus without Freaking Out* is a wonderful resource for learning to do just that—in real conversations with real people. This second edition is packed with practical advice on building authentic relationships, meeting people in their blessings and brokenness, and intentionally proclaiming what truly is the best news they'll ever hear. The small group discussion questions and 'Eight-Week Challenge' facilitate making this easy-to-read volume into a way of life."

—**Susan Booth**, professor of evangelism and missions, Canadian Southern Baptist Seminary and College

"I want to recommend to everyone the book, *Sharing Jesus without Freaking Out* as an excellent resource to strengthen your witness. Evangelism is more caught than taught, but it must be strengthened. This book will release your passion of making Christ known with simple, but solid principles of Scripture. We shouldn't freak out about sharing Christ; we should be Jesus followers, and this book will inspire you!"

—**Scott Dawson**, founder and CEO, Scott Dawson Evangelistic Association

"Most non-Christians have no idea what the gospel actually is. There are multiple obstacles causing this, but the greatest obstacles are in the hearts and minds of believers who rarely share the good news with people who need to hear. This is an important and extremely practical book for those who want to love God and their neighbors. Sharing Christ can be natural and normal in our lives with a little prayer, preparation, and practice. I will recommend this book to my seminary students."

—**Don Dent**, director, Kim School of Global Missions and Baker James Cauthen Professor of World Missions, Gateway Seminary

"As a pastor, nothing brings me more joy than when a member of my congregation introduces me to someone they have led to Christ. If there were one thing I yearn to see restored to the body of Christ it would be this, which makes this book all the more important. Sharing effectively with others is the most foundational skill of ministry and one of the essential—not to mention most exhilarating—disciplines of the Christian life. Hildreth and McKinion strip away the fear involved in evangelism and help people see that telling others about Jesus can be as normal as talking about kids, sports, or a favorite hobby. I cannot recommend this book highly enough."

—**J. D. Greear**, pastor, Summit Church, Raleigh-Durham, NC, and president, the Southern Baptist Convention

"I started reading this book because I was asked to write an endorsement. I continued reading it because it is really good and very practical. There are so many great concepts and practical suggestions in this book that I have struggled to write a brief endorsement that might encourage you to read it. For example, sharing the gospel should be as natural as sharing any other story. Be yourself and share from your strengths. You are a Christian, you have a story, you have relationships, you are all set. Evangelism is storytelling and everyone has a story. This book is about having a gospel conversation and not about repeating a canned presentation. Just immerse yourself in *that* story and allow the Spirit to guide. I love this book and I plan to use the ideas to assist me in telling *the* story."

—**Ken Hemphill**, special assistant to the president
and distinguished professor of Christian
studies, North Greenville University

"Scott Hildreth and Steven McKinion are to be commended for their new book, *Sharing Jesus without Freaking Out*. This book provides very simple tools for living a lifestyle of evangelism. While some books on evangelism overlook the message of the gospel, *Sharing Jesus* does not. I especially enjoyed appendix 2: Sharing the Story of the Gospel."

—**Thomas P. Johnston**, professor of evangelism, Midwestern
Baptist Theological Seminary, and secretary-treasurer,
Southern Baptist Professors of Evangelism Fellowship

"Scott Hildreth and Steve McKinion have written *Sharing Jesus without Freaking Out* to encourage believers who are nervous about evangelism with the hope that they can actually relax when it comes to personal evangelism. They reassure fearful, would-be, personal evangelists that they can confidently share Jesus with unbelievers, naturally and casually, in the context of conversations and relationships."

—**Matt Queen**, associate dean, Fish School of Evangelism
and Missions, associate professor of evangelism, and
L. R. Scarborough Chair of Evangelism ("the Chair of
Fire"), Southwestern Baptist Theological Seminary

"Relational evangelism is often maligned in evangelical circles and perhaps for good reason. Far too often the emphasis in relational evangelism is upon the 'relational' and not the 'evangelism.' In this volume, Hildreth and McKinion strike a healthy Great Commission balance. They help Christ-followers understand that personal relationships are a natural pathway for gospel conversation. Therefore, be a friend, share the gospel; there's nothing to fear."

—**Chuck Register**, executive leader, church planting and missions partnerships, Baptist State Convention of North Carolina

"Most believers have had some sort of 'freak out' moment when it comes to evangelism—whether that's freaking out about when to start a gospel conversation, how to share the message clearly, or what to do when we encounter objections or hostility. McKinion and Hildreth provide a wholesome and intelligent approach to evangelism that will not only help overcome barriers, but also inspire eagerness in sharing the message of Christ. I am thankful to have this book in hand, and I look forward to putting it into the hands of others who want to become more passionate and effective in sharing the gospel."

—**Stephen Rummage**, senior pastor, Quail Springs Baptist Church, Oklahoma City, OK

"In a day when fewer believers are engaging others in gospel conversations, I'm for any solid resource that will provide encouragement and practical tools to confidently lead them to practice the spiritual discipline of evangelism. Scott Hildreth and Steve McKinion have winsomely written a practical tool that does just that. In a fast-paced life that feels too busy or an apprehensive life that feels too afraid to evangelize, Hildreth and McKinion show believers how they can take advantage of the small everyday opportunities the Lord orchestrates for them and how they can use the narrative of Scripture and their testimonies to engage in effective evangelism for the glory of God."

—**Ed Stetzer**, Billy Graham Chair of Church, Mission, and Evangelism and dean, School of Mission, Ministry, and Leadership, Wheaton College

SHARING JESUS

without

FREAKING OUT

SECOND EDITION

SHARING
JESUS

without
FREAKING
OUT

EVANGELISM
the Way You Were
Born to Do It

D. SCOTT HILDRETH
& STEVEN A. McKINION

ACADEMIC
NASHVILLE, TENNESSEE

Published by B&H Academic
Nashville, Tennessee

ISBN: 978-1-5359-8218-4

Dewey Decimal Classification: 248.5
Subject Heading: CHRISTIAN LIFE \ EVANGELISTIC WORK \
WITNESSING

Graphics courtesy of Keegan Pierce.

Printed in the United States of America

3 4 5 6 7 8 9 10 BTH 26 25 24 23 22

This book was written with our own kids in mind: Rachel, Jacob, Lachlan, Blakely, and Harrison. Our hope is that God uses them, and many others of their generation, as witnesses of his grace.

Contents

Acknowledgments

We are both indebted to so many people for the production of this book. First, we are thankful to Danny Akin, president of Southeastern Seminary, and Bruce Ashford, the provost, for helping create an institution single-mindedly focused on the Great Commission: Jesus's call to join him in the work of seeing people reconciled to God.

Chris Thompson and Jim Baird at B&H Academic saw value in a second edition of *Sharing Jesus without Freaking Out* and gave us the opportunity to produce it. Many thanks to the entire team of editors at B&H who helped make the book what it is.

Christy Thornton and John Lewis read every word of each draft. Where we were wise enough to follow their suggestions, the book became better than it would ever have been without them. They were both immensely helpful in crafting the book as well as in smoothing the rough edges.

Our friends and pastors, J. D. Greear, David Sims, and Marty Jacumin, who exemplify the "evangelistic" pastor, laboring to teach Christians to faithfully share Jesus without freaking out. While we have taught these ideas to thousands of people, their feedback and suggestions have shaped our thinking and our teaching. We are especially grateful to them.

All of the people mentioned above helped with the development of this book. However, the highest earthly acknowledgments go to our wives, Lesley and Ginger. Their patience, help, and support made us the men we are today; they made this book possible.

Introduction

There are millions of people who do not know Jesus. Some of them are your friends. They are the point of this book.

Sharing Jesus with someone else is . . . what's the right wording for it?

Does it *freak you out*?

If so, we understand. You probably wouldn't equate it with the kind of "freaking out" that makes you want to run screaming to get away from something that's suddenly scared or startled you. It's more like the reluctance you might feel if you were to think about asking your boss for a raise. It's one of those conversations you'd do just about anything to avoid because it makes you so uncomfortable. What if the person demeans you? Or gets mad at you? You can't know ahead of time where this thing is likely to go.

So it's the awkwardness of it, the potential for embarrassment—not knowing exactly how to do it, not being sure you can answer all the questions somebody might ask you, not wanting to offend or be thought of as weird, narrow, or pushy. You certainly don't want to be grouped in with those radicals on social media who equate their Christianity with their political positions.

It's *all* of those fears, isn't it? Of course it is.

But it doesn't have to be. (And we intend to start convincing you of this in the first chapter.) In fact, if we could boil down into a single line apiece all the principles behind all eight chapters of this book, here's what we plan on helping you discover about sharing Jesus with others.

1

- Evangelism doesn't have to be uncomfortable.
- You're under no pressure to prove anything.
- It really just amounts to having a conversation . . .
- and almost any context provides the opportunity for evangelism.
- You can spot these opportunities when you listen . . .
- because people talk about what's best for them.
- So think of evangelism as building a relationship with someone . . .
- and intentionally planning to share Jesus as a part of everyday living.

Sharing Jesus with another person is really no more daunting or complicated than that. And since we believe you're already fully on board with the last of these eight principles (or else you wouldn't be here to begin with), there's no doubt this is something you can do.

The book you're about to read is not a comprehensive theology of evangelism or the methods by which that theological message is communicated. Our goal is simply to show you what evangelism looks like when it's part of your ordinary, everyday conversations. We want to demystify sharing Jesus until it's as natural to you as working your job, practicing a favorite hobby, or engaging in any other kind of daily activity.

Wouldn't that be great?

You've probably thought the day would surely come when sharing your faith would finally get easier. Problem is, that day never just shows up. But whether you're a teenager or senior adult, a PTA member or CEO, a parent, even a pastor—because, yes, we know it can freak pastors out too!—you are holding a tool that can make that day a reality for you. In the next hundred pages or so, we intend to show you how to make sharing the gospel a commonplace part of your lifestyle.

Without all the *freaking out* part.

{ CHAPTER 1 }

Evangelism Doesn't Have to Be Uncomfortable

"We are unable to stop speaking about what we have seen and heard."

—Acts 4:20

Principle #1

You have all you need to begin sharing
Jesus with other people right now.

Y ou do things every day that, to many of the rest of us, would be daunting to the point of impossible. Maybe you run your own business, or hang drywall, or fly airplanes, or craft floral arrangements, or care for cancer patients, or teach preschool. It's something you do routinely, all the time, without freaking out.

Why?

Because you learned how to do it. More accurately, you learned you *could* do it.

There was a time, of course, when you couldn't. None of us, when we picked up our first book, for example, knew how to read. When we sat behind the steering wheel of a car for the first time, we didn't yet know how to drive.

Name some of the many insurmountable challenges you've faced in life: figuring out high school algebra, remodeling your kitchen or bathroom, interviewing for your first real job. The challenge seemed overwhelming. You weren't sure you could do it. And yet you did. You learned a second language. You taught yourself to sew. You graduated from college. You ran a marathon. You did it!

So you have a history of accomplishing things, of becoming adept at things that you once couldn't do at all, until now you can do them quite naturally, with ease—or, if not with ease, at least proficiently. Those tasks don't scare you to death anymore. You may even be genuinely looking forward to your next chance at doing them again.

Why should evangelism be any different?

Here's why: likely, somewhere along the way, you were taught a style of evangelism that made the idea of talking with other people about the best news in the history of humanity(!) feel somehow uncomfortable. You knew you should do it. You even *wanted* to do it. You loved the thought of an unbeliever being captured by the message of Christ you shared and then putting their faith in him. Of the thousands of Christians we've known and taught throughout the years, seldom have we met anyone who refused to share Jesus because they didn't think it was important.

But stop us if what we're saying isn't true. Tell us evangelism hasn't become equated in your mind with things that you find to be highly unpleasant, unnatural, uncomfortable.

For one thing, it's been made to feel like public speaking. And almost everybody hates public speaking. According to a Gallup study, the only thing greater than the fear of public speaking for today's adults is the fear of snakes—more than fear of heights, fear of flying, fear of spiders, fear of tight spaces, fear of anything.[1] Most of us would almost prefer dangling from the ledge of a tall building than to try giving the kind of talk we perceive as being a gospel presentation.

In addition, evangelism training has often been led by aggressive, extroverted instructors who, if they weren't leading witnessing classes and seminars, would make really good salespeople, motivational speakers, or multilevel-marketing professionals. Each of these careers, of course, is noble work, but let's face it: they typically require a certain kind of temperament or skill set in order for someone to be successful at them. And if that kind of person is not you—like that person is neither one of us—you'll likely feel inadequate for the job. Whenever the evangelism method that's being taught doesn't work for every personality type, a lot of people are sure to feel a little freaked out.

Finally, many of the most prominent forms of evangelism training through the years have been heavy on techniques, strategies, and scripted questions that may work fine for "professional" Christians, but not for regular believers interacting with regular people. Plans like these are often not natural to implement. They mostly just feel intimidating. And so, rather than being an encouragement to go out there and share Jesus with others, such methods can unintentionally quash enthusiasm for evangelism by causing people to think they must be doing it all wrong, which only makes them more apprehensive and avoidant, more easily tongue-tied in trying to carry it out.

If this describes you, we feel your pain. The two of us have spent three decades in some of the same meetings and training sessions, learning about methods for sharing the gospel. Some have been helpful, but we have come out of a lot of those

---

[1] Geoffrey Brewer, "Snakes Top List of Americans' Fears," Gallup, March 19, 2001, http://Gallup.com/poll/1891/snakes-top-list-americans-fears.,aspx.

sessions thinking, *That can't be the ONLY way to do evangelism!* Sometimes a method can seem forced or so complicated that normal Christians can't imagine themselves ever actually sharing Jesus with anyone, much less a close friend or family member.

But evangelism doesn't need to feel this way, where it's one of those things you hate being expected to do. The first step toward becoming a Christian who shares Jesus without freaking out is to understand evangelism in a way that removes complications and makes it feel natural.

This book is about that kind of evangelism.

And in this chapter, we want to give you the first part of it. The type of evangelism we'll be describing for you focuses on what you already possess simply by virtue of being a Christian. Or, as our Principle #1 says it, *You have all you need to begin sharing Jesus with other people right now.*

Think of it in three broad categories:

1. Evangelism is an overflow of the Christian life.

The most important requirement for learning to share Jesus is not a winsome personality, a tight presentation, or a well-developed plan. The main ingredient for sharing Jesus the way you were born to share him is simply a genuine relationship with him.

Evangelism happens within the regular rhythm of living with Christ yourself, of being an active participant in the gospel. The more you know him and enjoy him, the more you'll enjoy sharing his story. When Jesus is the central figure of your life—when he determines what you value most, what brings you joy, what stirs your sense of justice, and what you'd fight to the death to protect—he will be what you talk about. If you'll focus on just being a Christian, the ease of casually communicating Christ will start to come naturally.

Your identity in Christ is the basic starting point for evangelism—and yet it's so easy to forget.

There are three reasons many of us forget the importance of our relationship with Jesus: distractions, difficulties, and disobedience. We live in a fast-paced society, and the circumstances of life can distract us from the gracious work of God in our hearts. We live in a broken world filled with suffering; it's easy to allow difficulties to draw us away from his goodness. Finally, we all know the reality of our own sin. Our lives can be summarized as the apostle Paul summarized his:

> I do not understand what I am doing, because I do not practice what I want to do, but I do what I hate. . . . For I know that nothing good lives in me, that is, in my flesh. For the desire to do what is good is with me, but there is no ability to do it. For I do not do the good that I want to do, but I practice the evil that I do not want to do. (Rom 7:15, 18–19)

Our own shortcomings and failures can cause doubts about who we really are. In the face of these facts, it is important to always remember this:

> You are [part of] a chosen race, a royal priesthood, a holy nation, a people for his own possession, so that you may proclaim the praises of the one who called you out of darkness into his marvelous light. (1 Pet 2:9)

As a Christian, you enjoy a relationship with God that he has designed for you. You are a chosen part of his kingdom. You've been "rescued" from the kingdom of darkness and delivered "into the kingdom of the Son he loves" (Col 1:13). You belong to God and are known by him as his beloved son or daughter.

But there's more. Having been delivered from your sins, you've become part of a royal priesthood, a job description that dates back to the rescue of the Hebrews from Egypt (Exod 19:6). God's purpose for delivering Israel wasn't simply to take them out of slavery, any more than his saving of you was solely to forgive you of your sins. He wanted his ancient people to enjoy and experience the kind of relationship with him that would give them the opportunity of helping others enjoy him as well. And so he declared them not just a kingdom *with* priests but a kingdom *of* priests.

Priests connect people to God. Priests share messages of hope and help with others. And you, as one of his modern-day priests, are in an ideal position to tell people how truly wonderful your God is.

You're someone who knows from firsthand experience that the God of the Bible is not a terrifying God who's out to hurt people, even incredibly sinful people. You know that the real enemy of humankind is sin, not God, and that God's desire is to *save* people from their sins, giving them a new heart, a new hope, a new home.

It is this saving work, which God has done in your own heart, that equips you "so that you may proclaim the praises of the one who called you out of darkness into his marvelous light" (1 Pet 2:9).

Now this discovery alone, we realize, is probably not enough to put you at total ease in sharing Jesus. You may be thinking you need a lot more than that. But God hasn't left you all alone down here to figure out how to share him without any help. God himself indwells you through his Holy Spirit, who guides you, informs you, and empowers you to be his faithful witness in the world (Acts 1:8).

As if the knowledge of God's presence with you is not enough, remember that God has given you even more: *the gift of prayer*, which provides you opportunity to communicate (and even commune) with God as he empowers you to become his unlikely vehicle for spreading the gospel.

Prayer, first of all, is able to shape your attitude about *God's mission*. The praying Christian is one whose mindset stays anchored on spiritual matters and who increasingly thinks rightly about God. When you practice a lifestyle of prayer, you naturally become more sensitive to gospel concerns, which opens your spiritual eyes to witnessing opportunities you might otherwise miss.

Next, prayer shapes your attitude about *people*. Through prayer, you begin to see people as God sees them. Suddenly your neighbor is no longer just the person who lives on your street or in your apartment complex; he or she is someone for whom Jesus died and was raised from the dead. Praying for specific people grows your love for them enough that you *want* to share your Savior with them.

And so, because of who you are, you're already enlisted and empowered to do this. The Holy Spirit within you will guide you into conversations, open doors for gospel interaction, and use those encounters to bring people to new life in salvation.

Like the priests of old, you—as a member of this royal priesthood—have been tasked with and equipped for delivering a message of God's love, mercy, and grace to others. Not everyone will want to hear what you have to say, of course, nor will they all believe that the message applies to them. But your responsibility is simply the sharing. And everything you need for doing it is right there inside of you.

2. Evangelism is storytelling, and every Christian has a story.

You may have been a Christian for many years, or perhaps you're relatively new to the Christian faith. You may also have tried any number of different methods or strategies to help you be better at evangelism. But establishing a lifestyle of sharing Jesus does not require new tools or techniques or even new skills. Think of it as simply retelling a story—something you already do all the time.

The reason you can tell a story, whether it's the story of your first kiss or the story of your child's first steps, is because you *know* those stories. That's all it really takes to be able to share them. Being personally familiar with a story that you want to tell is why you can so vividly describe scenes from your childhood to your kids, or recount the events of your workday to your spouse, or jump into nearly any conversation on any topic by interjecting a story that connects with whatever's being talked about.

Storytelling. That's what evangelism really is. The gospel at its heart is the story of God reaching out to the people he made and enabling them to live in right relationship with him because of what Jesus Christ has done on their behalf. Every Christian knows this story. *You* know this story. Or if you don't feel that you know it well enough to articulate it fluently, we'll be talking about it so much throughout this book that by the time you reach the end, we trust you'll believe that you can.

You also know your *own* story, your personal pilgrimage that led you to faith in Christ, as well as the story of what his grace continues to accomplish in your life even now. Evangelism, the way he uniquely made you to do it, involves that story too.

Think about the ministry of Jesus. As he taught, he told stories. He told stories about weddings and farming and tending sheep. He told stories about rich people and poor people, about faithful people and foolish people. He took ordinary circumstances that everybody in his day understood, and he used those stories to talk about the eternal God. And most people loved it.

Because everybody enjoys hearing stories.

What they *don't* enjoy is a sales pitch . . . which you don't enjoy giving anyway, and which you probably aren't internally wired to deliver. Few things are more uncomfortable to most of us than giving a canned evangelistic spiel that ends with a demand for a response. Good thing, then, that sharing Jesus is not about honing a sales technique. It's simply about retelling a story. *This* story. *These* stories.

Too many Christians continue to equate evangelism with a prepackaged presentation, or with asking and answering a particular set of questions, or with trying to win a theological debate. One of the reasons Christians avoid engaging in evangelism, or typically avoid the topic of religion altogether in polite company, is because they fear the resulting discussion will deteriorate into an argument. Some people love arguments; most people loathe them.

When you act like a telemarketer toward non-Christians, you can expect to get a predictable result: hang-ups. But when you simply view evangelism as storytelling—telling the story of the gospel and the story of God's work in your life *through* that gospel—the fear starts to go away. No longer do you feel responsible for proving a point. You're not arguing for why your views are correct and why opposing views are mistaken. And you're certainly not suggesting that becoming a Christian will instantly solve anyone's problems.

Sharing Jesus doesn't need to be uncomfortable, unnatural, and forever confined to that dreaded emotional space between awkward and terrifying. It can actually be as natural as sharing any other story from any other part of your life. It's just another ordinary conversation with ordinary people. The way you already know how to do it.

3. Evangelism is relational, and every Christian has relationships.

When you (1) truly make God the main focus of your life as a Christian, and (2) recognize him as the main character in the story of the Bible, as we'll soon discuss in greater detail, you can then (3) make him the main focus of your conversations with others. You can begin to weave Jesus naturally into the fabric of your ordinary relationships, just as his gospel is woven into the fabric of your being. Your love for *him* joins together with your love for *them*—your friends, your family, your coworkers, even your care and compassion for total strangers—so that as you're going about your everyday business, you find yourself entering into the privilege of sharing the story of God's grace with them.

And you don't even need to go out looking for people to share him with, because they're already there.

Your life is a line that continually intersects with others every day. Depending on your current season or situation, you

routinely experience an assortment of the following connections: you wake up next to your spouse in the morning; you
have breakfast with your kids; you wave hello to your neighbor
as you walk down the driveway; you chat with the cashier at
the grocery store; you spend an hour in a meeting with some
of your work associates; you visit with other parents while your
children take a dance class; you hang out at the lake with
friends. Each of these encounters—and all the many others
like them—represents an intersection. Granted, none of them
on its own may seem to contain anything overtly spiritual. But
what if they do?

We ought to see *every* encounter as special, not because
each one is sure to end up with someone becoming a Christian
or even with an opportunity to share the gospel. It's special simply because you're living that moment alongside an individual
whom God has put in relationship with you (whether temporar-
ily or long-term)—a person he loves, someone who has a place
in his story already.

And this will always be the case. All the time.

Each of your current and future relationships exists as a
ready, natural, ongoing conduit for the gospel. God, through
Christ's work, has brought you into relationship with him, and
along the way he's also brought you into relationship with others. *Many* others. This is God's plan for the progress of the gospel, whether you're encouraging your family or fellow believers
in their faith, or introducing the non-Christians in your life to
the story of God's love for them.

Either way, your only real job is to enjoy these relationships that are already yours. Christ has achieved everything
required to advance his gospel; you now get the opportunity
to enjoy his work and how he chooses to do it. It's as if someone has bought you a piano and given you all the skill and
resources you need for playing it. It's time now to just sit down
on that bench, beside whomever he plops into your life today,
and play away!

Start by simply determining that your purpose in life is to participate with God in the progress of the gospel, and then begin seeing your daily encounters with others as special opportunities to bless and encourage them. No encounter is without value if you believe the story of the gospel includes everyone. The non-Christian barista who serves you at the counter isn't likely to become a believer merely because you always come into the coffee shop with a friendly smile. But each of your interactions with him or her could contribute toward opening up this person to gospel conversations, whether with you or with someone else.

It's what these relationships of yours are for. Random encounters become gospel encounters when you live Christianly within the relationships you already have. And look around: you certainly don't lack for relationships.

Act Naturally

You're a Christian.

You have a story.

You have relationships.

You are all set then. Principle #1: *You have all you need to begin sharing Jesus with other people right now.*

We repeat: despite what you may have been led to believe, evangelism does not mean attending another conference, learning a new approach, or gaining new insights into people. Your ability to casually communicate Christ—to share Jesus without freaking out—means just being yourself, a child of God. You may be an extroverted Christian or an introverted Christian; either way, you're a Christian. And that's enough. Evangelism doesn't require you to change who you are.

Do you like to talk to strangers? Then talk to strangers. Are you scared even to look at people you don't know? Then don't look at people you don't know. It's not an accident that God made you with your own particular temperament. In fact, living out your personality is the most natural way for you to display his work in your life. Remember, you're not signing up to be a salesperson; you're just signing up to live as a Christian.

So be content being yourself—with your own style, traits, interests, and relationships—because that is what God has given you. Your genes, your environment, your experiences, your education—each of them play a role in your approach to evangelism.

Do you love movies? Music? Art? College football? Then just roll with how God has formed you and where he's taken your passions. Embrace them fully and engage them for the sake of Christ and the progress of the gospel. Leverage your inherent skills, abilities, and predilections as means of establishing authentic relationships with others. And once inside those relationships, use them to talk about Jesus, the One who is *most* important to you.

Because if your faith matters to you—and we know it does—you'll naturally include something of the gospel story in your normal conversations. You won't need to manufacture those interactions or awkwardly infuse religion into your relationships. It'll all happen naturally, as God works through you, through what matters most to you.

In 1 Thess 2, Paul reminded the young believers in the church at Thessalonica that he and his companions had not used coercive means or other crafty approaches to try convincing people that they should become Christians: "We never used flattering speech, as you know, or had greedy motives—God is our witness—and we didn't seek glory from people, either from you or from others" (vv. 5–6). After all, Paul wasn't looking for personal followers or leading a cult; he was only looking to tell people some good news.

The same is true of you. Whenever you're telling your friends about something, you don't use unnatural tactics to do it. You just tell them. You tell them with your life, with your actions, with your stories: "Here's what I did this weekend";

"Here's where I went yesterday"; "Here's an interesting thing I learned recently." Why make sharing Jesus with them any more complicated than that?

In his excellent book *Joy for the World,* author Greg Forster puts it this way:

> If they [people outside the church] encounter Christianity through our efforts to leverage secondary assets (politics, scholarship, worldview, . . . emotions, causes), they will not encounter the joy of God. But when they see that the total Christian life makes a radical difference in homes, workplaces, and communities, they will want to know why. Then they will know that the joy of God is a real thing. Then they will know there is a real supernatural power working in the lives of Christians.[2]

God has situated your life within a web of contexts. You have a home, a neighborhood, a city, a workplace, and a group of friends who likely possess many of the same interests as you. If you'll simply participate within these contexts in sincere and genuine ways, without feeling the need to force things, you will naturally exhibit the gospel through your ordinary interactions. Be a good family member, a good friend, a good Little League coach, a good worker . . . a good member of your own context, right where you live. And then watch God create opportunities for you to make much of the grace of Christ.

What the two of us hope to see today are more Christians like those unnamed believers in Acts 11:19–23 who planted the gospel deeply in Antioch, the fourth-largest city in the first-century Roman Empire. We need more Christians like the

---

[2] Greg Forster, *Joy for the World: How Christianity Lost Its Cultural Influence and Can Begin Rebuilding It* (Wheaton, IL: Crossway, 2014), 94.

ones described by Michael Green in his book *Evangelism in the Early Church:*

> In contrast to the present day, when Christianity is highly intellectualized and dispensed by professional clergy to a constituency increasingly confined to the middle class, in the early days the faith was spontaneously spread by informal evangelists and had its greatest appeal among the working class.[3]

The primary means of the gospel's early spread came through evangelism done in "the marketplace," through Christians engaged in everyday conversations with their friends and neighbors.[4] The evangelists of that era were primarily average Christians who retold the story of God's work in reconciling the world to himself. By sharing that story from within the contexts of their normal relationships, they took an active role in the mission. They became, as Paul referred to the Christians in Philippi, "partners" in the advance of the gospel (Phil 1:7; see also "partnership" in v. 5). They grabbed hold of what was already in their hands—their faith, their stories, their network of relationships—and they used it all to share Jesus throughout the rhythms of each day.

Christian evangelism can always be enhanced, of course, by churches putting on big events or launching big programs, inviting the whole community to attend. But nothing will ever be more effective—more natural—than ordinary, everyday Christians building genuine, lasting, individual friendships through which others can both see and hear the gospel.

---

[3] Michael Green, *Evangelism in the Early Church*, rev. ed. (Grand Rapids: Eerdmans, 2004), 175.

[4] For examples from early Christianity, see *Life and Practice in the Early Church: A Documentary Reader*, ed. Steven A. McKinion (New York: NYU Press, 2001), 115–50.

And don't ever think of it as something you can't do. *Because you can.*

The same gospel story that changed your life can give you the ability to move beyond your insecurities and talk about Jesus. No doubt about it. So be encouraged, because nothing you do for God is done alone. The Father sees you, the Son compels you, and the Spirit guides you and empowers you.

So as we conclude this chapter and look forward to where we're going from here, we encourage you to begin regularly praying a short prayer like this one:

> *God, I know you love people. Give me an opportunity today to help someone see your love for them and hear of how they can enjoy your work in Jesus Christ. Give me the boldness to talk with them about Jesus. Amen.*

Let's do it.

CHAPTER 2

Evangelism Is Storytelling

I passed on to you as most important what I also received: that Christ died for our sins according to the Scriptures, that he was buried, that he was raised on the third day according to the Scriptures.

—1 Corinthians 15:3–4

Principle #2

You don't have to prove the claims of Christianity, just present them clearly.

D o you like to talk politics? Maybe yes, maybe no. But if you do, you probably bring up the subject only when you're talking with somebody who already shares your views and opinions. Because if you don't know for sure what a person thinks or where that person stands on political matters, conversations can get really uncomfortable really fast.

That's because politics, by its nature, involves what we think is *right*. It speaks to people's ideas about how a society should function. And anyone who disagrees with those ideas is *wrong*.

Politics divides people into camps according to their priorities, beliefs, and positions; the opposing side is often portrayed as the enemy or ignorant. For this reason, many of us tend to steer clear of politically charged conversations.

Unfortunately, many Christians avoid evangelism for the same reason. They think it requires debating about why Christianity is right and everyone else is wrong. And they're rarely in the mood for that kind of confrontation.

But we (the authors) want to encourage you to see evangelism differently.

Let's take our cues from people such as Paul, for example, in the way he shared Jesus in the ancient Greek city of Athens (Acts 17:16–34). He knew that his purpose in that particular moment and context was not to force his hearers to agree with him, but to share with them what was really true and then give them the opportunity to respond in faith.

We're told in this passage that the Athenian people loved learning and debating new ideas (v. 21), so they were open to hearing from this guy who'd arrived in town with something fresh to say. But when Paul stood up to address them (vv. 22–31), he did not talk about why his religion offered better answers to the questions of life than the ones advanced by their own religious philosophies. He instead seized on their desire to be religious. He started with their questions and need as he told a story—a story about their "Unknown God" (v. 23)—a story in which, perhaps to their surprise, they were already included as participants.

> From one man he has made every nationality to live over the whole earth and has determined their appointed time and the boundaries of where they live. He did this so that they might seek God, and perhaps they might reach out and find him, though he is not far from each one of us. For in him we live and move and

have our being, as even some of your own poets have said, "For we are also his offspring." (vv. 26–28)

Paul simply told them a story. He guided them through the grand narrative of Scripture (which we'll be distilling for you in the pages of this chapter). He told them the God of the Bible was personally interested in them by virtue of their being part of the human race he created. And Paul said God had made them for a purpose: the purpose of having a relationship with him.

Now Paul obviously believed all this to be true. He believed his words accurately presented the real nature of both God and humanity. And of course it *was* true. *Is* true. But the fact that he believed it to be true wasn't the point, just as it's not the point of our evangelism today. The purpose of evangelism is simply to retell the story of the gospel of Jesus Christ according to the written text of Scripture in a way that listeners can understand.

Evangelism is not about winning an argument.

Sure, there are certain contexts that call for lively debate. But in our experience, ordinary interactions with friends, family, coworkers, and others rarely require advanced apologetics. The difference between someone becoming a Christian or remaining an unbeliever isn't typically a matter of convincing them that Jesus was a real person. Or convincing them of *anything* for that matter. Your task is not to prove yourself right and the unbeliever wrong, as though the only reason they're not a Christian is because they have faulty information.

Always keep in mind Principle #2: *You don't have to prove the claims of Christianity, just present them clearly.*

And nothing does it better than telling a story.

Staying on Message

The gospel makes a large number of truth claims. It teaches us the truth about God, the world, humankind, Jesus Christ;

in fact, the entire future of the universe. And none of these claims is insignificant. They are central to the Christian message . . . central because they are *true*. There's no such thing as subjective Christian truth that is "true for you" if you happen to believe in Jesus.

But what difference does the truthfulness of Christianity make if no one understands its message? And why would arguing with someone help that person receive it any better? Religious arguments only succeed at distancing and distracting people from the central message of the gospel.

In other words, evangelism is less argument and more explanation. If you have a coworker who rejects your belief that the Bible is the Word of God, you may never be able to justify your views on Scripture so that he or she agrees with you. But you can still accurately share with them what the Bible says about Jesus. You won't be forcing belief on them; you'll simply be working to ensure they understand exactly what they're turning away from, if they decide to persist in saying no to him.

Imagine the following conversation, for instance, between a new Christian and a member of his family. A man tells his sister that he's become a follower of Christ, and she can't believe it. *My brother? Religious? No way!* The first time it comes up in conversation, she starts challenging him on some of the Christian claims she finds absurd: the virgin birth, a man who walks on water, a man who came back from the dead.

Her brother now has a decision to make.

Let's say he goes for the option of arguing against each of these doubts his sister has raised, using sound, logical, historical defenses of his own positions to show her why she's wrong. And let's say he does it well enough that he wins her over. She actually comes around to accepting his opinion that Jesus was a real man, that he could theoretically have been born of a virgin, and probably did rise from the dead. Is she now a Christian, merely by virtue of believing these facts? Of course not.

But what if instead the brother says something like this: "I know you have a number of reasons for not believing in Christ. And that's fine. But I do want to be sure you at least understand what being a Christian actually means. Because even though you may decide to *dismiss* the Christian gospel, which is your prerogative, you can't *change* the Christian gospel."

From here he proceeds to tell his sister the story—how God demonstrated his love by sending Jesus into the world. He talks about how sin separated humanity from God, and how faith in Jesus brings us back into relationship with him. No argument. Just a summary of what God has done for us in Christ.

If she accepts the truth about *this*—which she much more likely could—and if she agrees that she's a sinner in need of a Savior and believes in Jesus, is she a Christian now? She certainly is.

Conversion comes only through hearing, with understanding, the gospel of Jesus Christ. Evangelism is not about winning a debate; evangelism is about helping people understand the means by which they can be saved. The goal is not to show non-Christians they're wrong about everything—about God, Jesus, the Bible, sin, or anything else. Evangelism is the announcement of what God has done for all of us, and how each of us can enjoy the fruit of that work.

Tell that story clearly, and you'll be sharing Jesus well.

Story Basics

Stories are everywhere. They're common in our culture. In *all* cultures. People think in terms of stories. They live out stories. Communities are built around shared stories as much as around shared experiences. People read books; they watch movies; they attend the theater. They constantly tell stories to themselves and others because storytelling is wired into our DNA. We can't get enough of them. *We love stories.* And so, when you present the gospel as a story, you're speaking a language that people already understand.

Stories come in all shapes and sizes, but every story seems to fit within only a handful of major categories that storytellers use. Here are three you'll instantly recognize.[1]

1. Boy Meets Girl. The classic romance story. A guy and girl meet. They experience chemistry between them. Their first encounter typically involves an element of conflict (or else the story would be short and boring). Also, in most cases, one or both of the characters, despite being drawn toward the other, is not interested in pursuing love at this time or is not free to do so. Maybe they live in different cities. Maybe one of them is already involved in a relationship. The story, then, is how they overcome the various obstacles to their love.

2. Man Falls into a Hole. This plot type, sometimes called "Overcoming the Monster," begins with the protagonist doing well—everything's going fine in his life—until he meets with a predicament of some sort. The problem he faces may be some*thing* or some*one*, but the resulting situation causes him distress; and he must find a way to deal with it or get out of it. Usually, though, he can't save himself without help, so a host of supporting characters is needed to come to his aid, even as other characters—antagonists—stand in his way.

3. Rags to Riches. Unlike the "Man Falls into a Hole" plot-line, where a character's world is upended by a life-altering circumstance, this type of story opens with the protagonist already experiencing a desperate situation. Stories such as

---

[1] For an encyclopedic look at seven fundamental plotlines, see Christopher Booker, *The Seven Basic Plots: Why We Tell Stories* (London: Continuum, 2004). Booker identifies Overcoming the Monster, Rags to Riches, the Quest, Voyage and Return, Comedy, Tragedy, and Rebirth. He notes the best stories combine several of these plots; for instance, Tolkien's *The Lord of the Rings* trilogy combines six of the seven (excluding only comedy).

"Cinderella" come to mind—a young woman dealing with difficult relationships and other restraints on her ability to realize her ambitions and achieve what she wants in life.

You get the idea. And the point is, *everybody* gets the idea. Everybody understands the language of story. As you look at just these three basic plotlines, can't you see how the gospel dovetails right into them?

We can complicate evangelism when we use a canned presentation or artificially construct other ways of sharing a plan for salvation.

For instance, when we communicate the gospel as mainly a listing of facts about Christianity or benefits that Christianity offers. It is possible to present the gospel the same way a restaurant menu lists appetizers and entrees. Is the menu helpful? Sure, but only as a collection of information about what items the kitchen is able to provide.

When we limit evangelism to little more than benefit statements, we make it sound impersonal. Rather than merely presenting a menu of information about Christianity, we must learn to wrap its benefits and truths in the broader narrative of the Bible.

The Bible is not a collection of statements about God, meant to be boiled down to memorable bullet points. It's the story of a living, personal God seeking relationship with real-life human beings. In evangelism, we're trying to help people understand who this God is. And just as a menu doesn't tell you much, if anything, about the restaurant's owner, its chef, or its wait staff, any kind of evangelism that only highlights Christianity's truth claims or benefits doesn't compel people to know the God of the Bible.

Here's another way to complicate the gospel mission: when we primarily present the Bible as a handbook of personal advice, the place people go for the answers to how they should live. Want to have a happy marriage? Want to know how to better manage your money? Want to be a great leader? The Bible can show you, right?

Maybe, but that's not the main function of Scripture, nor is it what draws people more deeply into it so that they want to know God personally and live in relationship with him. They can live their lives for greater purposes than mere self-improvement.

Here's yet another complication we often add into our witnessing: asking questions no one else is asking. While the two of us are genuinely grateful for the various plans, programs, and methods of evangelism that have been taught through the years, we've observed that many of them are designed to work in contexts where people share a common worldview—one in which everyone possesses basic familiarity with biblical teaching.

This is especially true of a witnessing method that encourages you to start up a conversation with someone by asking a question that assumes belief in God, heaven, or a common understanding of sin and eternity. Problem is, fewer and fewer people these days know what they believe about God, heaven, or sin. They're just trying to live happy lives, build their careers, take care of their families. They're not thinking about much else. So when you lead with a question about something that doesn't really matter to them, you're probably only asking for an awkward, uncomfortable silence in return.

As always, a story will help us explain better what we mean. Consider this example.

I'm sure you have received a visit from someone coming to your door, aiming to convert you. They want you to become one of their number. Their sales pitch typically starts the same way every time: "Wouldn't you like to live in a world where people get along with one another and practice good family values?"

The right answer, of course, is yes. We would like to live in a world where people get along.

Imagine if someone answered the question, "No, I like the world just as it is."

That would certainly catch the questioner off guard . . . because in their minds *every* person would want to live in the kind of world they have described. But were you to tell them you don't really care if people get along with one another and do not believe the world can be improved, they wouldn't have an answer. Their presentation would fall apart because it's built entirely around a single concern. And when that concern doesn't connect to the person they're speaking with, there's not much of a pathway left for sharing the message.

Not everyone you meet is asking the kinds of questions that traditional gospel presentations are made to answer. Therefore, explaining the Bible to the non-religious people in your life requires a different approach.

If you really want to share Jesus—so that people can understand him and his message—pay attention to the way the stories of their lives intersect with God's story. Because Scripture tells that story. And it is a really good story.

When you tell it that way, people are a lot more likely to get the real message.

Telling the Story

Most Christians would love to know how to tell the story of the gospel in a way that's both winsome and accurate. So in this section, we want to give you an overview of the single biblical story. (Don't worry, this is easier than you might imagine. Because, hey, you already know the story. You're living it.)

In his excellent book on screenwriting, *The Anatomy of Story*, John Truby defines "story" this way: "A speaker tells a listener what someone did to get what he wanted and why."[2] Can the Bible be treated as a story, using this basic definition?

---

[2] John Truby, *The Anatomy of Story: 22 Steps to Becoming a Master Storyteller* (New York: Farrar, Straus and Giroux, 2008), 5.

Absolutely. The Bible is the "speaker." Its reader is the "listener." Whenever we read Scripture, we listen to the author speak. The only things left, then, are the final three elements: *who* did *what* and *why*.

1. "Someone"

You'll remember from school that the "someone" who's doing the main something in the story is the *protagonist*. All other characters fit into the story only because of how they relate in some way to this central figure.

In the Bible, *God* is the protagonist. The Bible is not the story of Noah, Abraham, Moses, David, Peter, Paul, and all the rest. They represent only the supporting cast. The "someone" is God.

But God is not just any supreme deity; he is a particular God. He is the God who created all things. He is the God who brought Israel out of Egypt, the God who revealed his name as Yahweh, and the God who came to earth as Jesus through the incarnation. We can say, then, that the Bible is a story about the God who is Jesus. *Jesus* is the "someone" in the story.

2. "What someone did to get what he wanted"

The second component of a story is the action the protagonist takes. *Someone did something.* So, the story of the Bible tells how God created a place for human beings to live; he created us with the capacity for being in right relationship with him; he became a human being himself in order to unite humanity to his own divine life; he died on the cross for our sins; he rose from the dead and now raises redeemed people from the dead, making us a new creation; he ascended to heaven so that his new creation could live forever in his presence.

The Bible is the story of God working in this way for the salvation of human beings. He has provided an opportunity for humanity to be reconciled to himself in Jesus Christ.

3. "And why"

Why did God work to bring salvation to humankind? What motivated him to do everything he did? One reason: *love.*

The God of the Bible has existed forever in an unbroken, loving relationship of Father, Son, and Spirit—the Trinity. And he has loved human beings from the beginning. *God loves us.* Scripture says, in fact, that "God is love" (1 John 4:8). Everything he does, he does as an expression of the love that he possesses within himself.

God was motivated to offer us the same love he knows as Father, Son, and Spirit. It's as though he said to himself, "My eternal, infinite love is so great, so incredible, that I want to share it with someone else." And so he created people who could enjoy him and his love forever.

There's your *who, what,* and *why.*

So let's put the story all together, hinging it on these most basic elements:

- "what someone"—God, through his Son, Jesus
- "did to get what he wanted"—he created people, a place for them to live, and a way for them to live in right relationship with him
- "and why"—because he loves them

As Paul said, "Christ died for our sins *according to the Scriptures.*" He was "buried" and "raised" from the dead "*according to the Scriptures*" (1 Cor 15:3–4, emphases added). The centrality of Jesus's death and resurrection can be understood only in light of how his acts fit into the entire story arc of the Bible. These acts of Jesus only make real sense when we present them in relation to all the rest, as flowing out of this grand narrative that we all participate in as God's creation.

Consider Jesus's encounter with the disciples in Luke 24. He first met these two travelers on the road to Emmaus (v. 13).

You'll recall that they didn't recognize him at first; he seemed to be only a stranger who'd walked up and joined their animated discussion about "everything that had taken place" that week (v. 14)—the crucifixion of Jesus and now his reported resurrection.

"What is this dispute that you're having?" Jesus asked, to which one of them replied, "Are you the only visitor in Jerusalem who doesn't know the things that happened there in these days?"

"What things?" Jesus asked (vv. 17–19).

So, they told him. He listened. And after hearing their summarized account (vv. 19–24), Jesus interjected a bit of biblical perspective. He mentioned that these events had long been foretold in Scripture, asking, "Wasn't it necessary for the Messiah to suffer these things and enter into his glory?" (v. 26).

> Then beginning with Moses and all the Prophets, he interpreted for them the things concerning himself in all the Scriptures. (v. 27)

He fit the crucifixion and resurrection inside the larger story.

Later that evening, after Jesus had disappeared from their presence, and after this pair of disciples had rushed to find the Eleven and tell them whom they'd just seen and conversed with, Jesus suddenly appeared in the midst of them all (vv. 33–36). Again, his followers were amazed at what they were experiencing. Jesus had died. Now Jesus was alive. In fact, he was *right there*! How could this be? What did this mean?

Notice what Jesus said.

> "These are my words that I spoke to you while I was still with you—that everything written about me in the Law of Moses, the Prophets, and the Psalms must be fulfilled." (v. 44)

Then notice what he did.

> Then he opened their minds to understand the Scriptures. (v. 45)

The center of the gospel story is, yes, the death and resurrection of Jesus Christ. That's the heart of God's work for the salvation of sinful people. But in these passages, Jesus wanted his followers to see that the events of that one weekend were rooted in the Old Testament, and their significance would continue forward into the New and beyond. So in order to help them understand what they were seeing, he expanded their panorama to include the whole of Scripture. He told them his death and resurrection were part of an epic story that God had *always* been telling.

This is huge. Crucial.

Many of the people with whom you share Jesus are, at best, like the disciples on the road to Emmaus. They *think* they know what's going on. They *think* they know all that matters about Jesus, the cross, and the empty tomb. They've heard all about him. They've heard all about it. Okay.

But they've likely missed the real point of the story.

- They need to understand the gospel from the perspective of the entire Bible.
- They need to see the story of Jesus as bigger than just a man who lived in the first century and was crucified under Pontius Pilate.
- They need to learn that the beginning of the gospel story is not the first Christmas in Bethlehem but is Gen 1:1, when God created the world.
- They need to know that the end of the story is not when they die; it's when God raises from the dead all who are in Christ Jesus to live with him forever.
- Plus, they need to see that between the beginning and the end is a daily life to be lived, and within that life God desires for people to know his love and enjoy him.

It's a big, big, amazing story. The gospel begins with eternal love, and it ends with eternal love. It comprises hundreds of smaller narratives (Bible stories) as well as proverbs, songs, and instructions. But they're all masterfully woven together into a single *metanarrative*—one overarching, grand story.

Here it is—the story of the Bible—in all its grandeur: (1) Creation, (2) Provision, (3) Fall, and (4) Promise.

The Gospel as Story

1. CREATION: God created the entire universe and everything in it.

The Bible, and thus the gospel, begins with God's act of creation: "In the beginning God created the heavens and the earth" (Gen 1:1). This first statement of Scripture immediately tells us the *who* and *what* of the Bible story: "God created."

He created "the heavens and the earth." This literary device is what's known as a *merism,* meaning it uses both ends of the phrase as a way of referring to the entire thing. Not just to each extreme alone but to everything in between.

If someone were to say, for example, they'd looked "high and low" for a piece of lost jewelry, they mean they not only searched specifically *high* and specifically *low* but also everywhere in between. Or if a husband says he loves his wife "body and soul," he means he loves everything about her, with everything about him.

So when the Scripture says, "God created the heavens and the earth," it means he made everything that exists. Or as John reiterated in his Gospel, speaking of Jesus, "All things were created through him, and apart from him not one thing was created that has been created" (John 1:3). Paul also says, "Everything was created by him, in heaven and on earth, the visible and the invisible, whether thrones or dominions or rulers or authorities—all things have been created through him and for him" (Col 1:16). God made it all.

2. PROVISION: *God made the earth habitable for human beings, then made Adam and Eve and put them in a garden where he provided everything they needed for life.*

After God made everything, the Bible says he fashioned together a wonderful place filled with every provision a human being would need to survive and thrive. He made the trees capable of producing food without any effort on anyone's part. God, as a good heavenly Father, made a perfect dwelling place for humanity. He didn't miss a thing.

Then, after preparing it—this marvelous garden of Eden— he made the first human with his own hands, fashioning Adam from the dust of the land itself. He then made a female who was as equally human as the male. And here in this paradise, Adam and Eve could live each day in right relationship with God and with each other.

He made them "in his own image," the Bible says (Gen 1:27). Perfectly united with God. Not only did they have their human existence but also eternal life—God's type of life. They knew him and they knew his love for them. They could hear his voice and understand what he was saying. They had full supply. They had joyful companionship. They had total safety. They had every-thing good that any person could want. And all they needed to do to remain in this garden and enjoy God's life was to trust him and obey him. Through faith in God they could rest in him and experience his bountiful provision forever. If only . . .

3. FALL: *Adam and Eve sinned and had to leave the garden to live in the wilderness.*

Adam and Eve's decision to disobey, to trust in their own wisdom instead of God's wisdom, caused their exile from the garden of Eden. They forfeited both the place and the life that God had graciously given them.

Up until then, they'd been able to freely enjoy God's pro-vision. From that point forward, however, everything would require effort. The world would constantly be working against them. Their days would be hard, and their lives would be subject to disease and sorrow, ultimately to decay and death. Once outside the safety of the garden, Adam and Eve—as well as all humanity which is descended from them—would be left exposed to a fallen planet, to a fallen state of existence. Whereas in the garden the lion had lain down with the lamb, in the wilderness the lion would eat the lamb. Sin would be humankind's relentless enemy. Sin would bring destruction on them.

And yet . . .

4. PROMISE: God promised a Son who would make a way for them to return to the garden and have eternal life.

Do you see it as a story now? The greatest story of all stories? Immediately following Adam and Eve's sin and subsequent exile from the garden, God promised he would provide the means for them to return to that paradise. Just as he'd created an ideal place for them to live in the beginning, he would do it again—despite their sin, despite their fall.

This creation, though—this new creation—would take place through God's own Son coming to earth as a human himself, being born from the lineage of Adam and Eve. The God who'd *created* humanity would actually *become* humanity . . . would become one of us. And through his incarnation, he would live a sinless life, die an atoning death, then be raised from the dead as a re-creation of humanity.

Sin mars God's good creation, but cannot overcome it. The darkness does not overcome the Light (John 1:5). In the end, God ushers in a new creation in which his children live forever in the place he has made for them. Jesus promises this re-creation (John 14:3) and fulfills that promise (Revelation 21–22). The gospel is the complete and robust message of God's final defeat of sin and death through his remarkable creation of the new heavens and new earth.

And there you have it. The story of the gospel.

The greatest story in the universe.

A Story to Share

Once you start seeing the whole Bible as a story, the gospel becomes clearer than ever. You start thinking of evangelism as simply the retelling of that story. An *understandable* story.

In accurately retelling the story of the gospel, you are offering non-Christians the knowledge necessary for salvation. It's not just your opinion anymore. It's not the pressure of proving every claim of Christianity or having every answer to every conceivable spiritual question. Nor is it solely an account of your own religious experiences. Those, of course, are subject to being misunderstood, both by yourself and others.

Evangelism is retelling THE story—the grand story of the Bible—in which God created a place, created a people, and created a means for those people to enjoy him forever, even *after* we separated ourselves from him and found the world and our lives in such a mess.

Sharing Jesus means immersing yourself in THAT story—the story of the Bible—*participating* in that story and then *retelling* it to other people in a way that demonstrates how they, too, might participate in it. The *story*, not your presentation skill, becomes their entry point into what it means to be rightly related with God, just as God desires it and just as he has provided for it.

Conversion, of course, is a spiritual work that God alone is able to accomplish. Converting others is not your job. But the only way people can be converted—the only way they can be drawn to Christ through repentance and faith—is by "hearing" the gospel with understanding (Rom 10:14), the gospel that Scripture says is "the power of God for salvation" (Rom 1:16).

And you know that story already.

You just need to tell it.

{ CHAPTER 3 }

Evangelism Is Better When It's a Conversation

He reasoned in the synagogue with the Jews and with those who worshiped God, as well as in the marketplace every day with those who happened to be there.

—Acts 17:17

Principle #3

Gospel conversations are better for everyone.

Imagine the interior of a small brick storefront on the main street of a little town. The aroma of freshly ground coffee greets you the moment you open its door. Smooth jazz plays in the background, above the random whir of artisan countertop appliances and the hiss of steam rising from carefully crafted hot beverages. Tables and soft chairs are scattered about, seemingly without plan or purpose; there people sit talking with one another. You place your order, and soon your warm caffe latte waits for you at the end of the counter.

What would you call such a place?

Sounds to us like the setting of a wonderful friendship.

There's a reason why most first dates involve restaurants, coffee shops, or something similar. They're a great place for conversation. Starbucks and Seattle's Best, even Dunkin' Donuts and Tim Horton's, have made fortunes off of people's insatiable desire for relationships. Social media companies thrive on the same thing: the fact that people want, *need*, friends and interaction. Facebook, Snapchat, and Instagram now package shared photographs together as "Stories."

We all just tend to gravitate to places that facilitate conversations.

One social media platform, we noticed, recently began posting what it calls "Memories," where it pulls up some of the things we wrote a decade ago when we all were first learning how to communicate in virtual neighborhoods. How embarrassing to read them again. We cringe every time. Those early posts were so mechanical and impersonal, weren't they? Mostly just statements like, "Going to dinner with the fam."

What kind of nonsense is that? Mere information. Or *proclamation*, to use a word that sounds more at home in a book on evangelism.

It's not a conversation. It's not the kind of thing that builds a stronger relationship.

Thankfully, this type of social media stiffness and stiltedness has nearly died out. But why did it go away? The reason we quit talking like that is because information doesn't foster relationships. And one of the unwritten rules of relationships is this: *Don't just tell me what you did; tell me something that helps me know you better.*

Social media posts today are more like this: "Here's an article that helps explain why childhood cancer is so hard to treat." On the surface it may still sound like a statement. It neither asks a question nor evokes a response. And yet what it says includes us in a community with other people. By posting it, we've shared an interest of ours. We've addressed a concern we feel. We've contributed to our friendships. See the difference? A person who reads what we put out there may or may not go pull up the article we referenced, but they'll at least know we shared it as an ordinary part of relationship. (And we won't be calling them later to tell them where we're going for dinner, in case they were wondering!)

Relationships are built on conversations, not pronouncements.

And therefore we offer Principle #3: *Gospel conversations are better for everyone.*

Conversations versus Presentations

All the research coming out of our culture today reveals an increasing level of biblical illiteracy. Within this context, then, where people's definitions of terms such as *sin, God, salvation, faith, grace,* and so forth can vary widely, any kind of bullet-point, how-to approach to gospel sharing is more likely to result in confusion and apprehension than in faith and conversion. And since we all desire our unbelieving friends, family, and neighbors to become Christians, we want to be sure we communicate the gospel to them in a way they can understand.

That's why we introduced the concept of storytelling in the previous chapter. It's a way of helping people truly understand what the Bible is about. It's also a way for our evangelism to move away from a rigid gospel *presentation* toward a more natural gospel *conversation.*

Before we go any further, we should probably define what we mean by a gospel presentation. For us, a gospel presentation means leading a person toward faith by taking that person through a list of truth statements about God and his work.

Perhaps the classic example is what's commonly known as the "Roman Road" to salvation. It looks something like this:

1. You have sinned against God and need salvation (Rom 3:23).
2. God offers you salvation as a free gift (Rom 6:23).
3. God showed you his love by dying for your sins (Rom 5:8).
4. You must call out to Jesus for salvation (Rom 10:9–10).
5. You can have assurance of salvation by faith (Rom 10:13).

Anything wrong with that list? Of course not. Each statement is absolutely true. And many people have been genuinely converted through presentations just like this one. Perhaps even *you* came to Christian faith when someone shared Jesus with you in a similar fashion. So, we're not suggesting that a Roman Road-type presentation is a bad thing or doesn't have its place. *It does.* We hope we're clear on that.

Here's the problem, though. We know of hundreds of instances of people hearing a gospel presentation, praying a prayer, feeling assured of their salvation at the time, and yet walking away without ever again evidencing any true conversion to Christ. Granted, this bail-out dynamic, where someone accepts a message in the moment but appears to quickly abandon that commitment, is not exclusive to Christian evangelism. How many times in life do people listen to someone's sales pitch and agree to purchase whatever item or service they're being offered, only to regret or rethink their decision later? That happens all the time.

But especially when it comes to the gospel, we always want to avoid this response. We desire a genuine conversion, not a person's mere affirmation of the truth claims we have presented. If we were selling plastic containers, we'd do whatever it took to extract a "yes" from somebody. But evangelism is not selling a product. Evangelism is telling a story. No one who really cares about a person wants to trick them into believing the gospel. We want them to truly become Christians.

And therein lies the limitation of the presentation model. People are much more likely to gain a real understanding of the gospel—the kind that draws them into a lifetime of genuine faith—through an ongoing relationship and dialogue with a Christian rather than just through hearing a fifteen-minute presentation.

For the record, here are some differences we've recognized between gospel presentations and gospel conversations:

Presentation	Conversation
Begins with a Christian worldview	Begins with the other person's worldview
Assumes knowledge and understanding of Christian vocabulary	Assumes little knowledge or understanding of Christian vocabulary
Focuses on salvation as a legal transaction	Focuses on salvation as relational
Makes sense to people with a church background	Makes sense of Christianity to those outside the church too
Goal is to answer any questions with truth, with a focus on winning	Goal is to communicate information, striving for clarity of understanding
Requires an immediate decision	Leaves the door open for a decision at any time
Success equals a positive decision for Christ	Hopes for a positive decision, but success equals another conversation and an ongoing relationship

As we've said before, many evangelism training methods have focused on evangelism as a presentation. Start conversations with people as an entry point into a sales pitch; pretend to have a genuine interest in them; ask a few leading questions about their friends, their interests, their religious experiences; and then launch into a monologue about their sin and God's salvation. Finally, end with this question: "Is there any reason you would not like to be saved?"

But in gospel *conversations,* a Christian seeks to do more than simply get someone's attention long enough to present some pertinent facts about God. The goal of a conversation is not to share as little of the gospel story as necessary before closing the deal. We want them to know—to *really* understand— what the gospel is all about.

So, the conversation is an invitation to a relationship. An invitation to *more* conversations. And this, we find, is how the gospel hits home.

Less Monologue, More Dialogue

Go back to Acts 17 again—the account of Paul's ministry in Athens—and notice a crucial part of the story that's easy to miss. We imagine Paul standing in the middle of a huge crowd, preaching, which at first glance would seem to be an impersonal evangelistic encounter. More of a one-off presentation. But look closer and you'll see that's not the case.

In the days beforehand, Paul had actually worked to establish a relationship with the citizens of Athens. He had gone into the synagogue to initiate conversations with the Jews, as well as into the marketplace, talking "every day with those who happened to be there" (v. 17). He listened to their beliefs; he learned about their religious practices; he participated in the types of discussions that the Greek mind most admired. So by the time he stood to address the gathered crowd (vv. 22–31), he wasn't forcing a presentation of the gospel on them out of the blue. Rather, he was rejoining a conversation that he and they had already been engaged in.

And even *that* wasn't the end of it. The Bible says that some of the Athenians wanted to hear more after Paul's address, so the conversation continued. Some of them believed; others didn't (vv. 32, 34). But again, the model that's demonstrated there is instructive to us now. Paul was saying, in essence, "If you want to know more, let's keep talking." And that's what we should want too.

The question at the end of a canned evangelistic presentation is, "Wanna buy or not? What can I do to make you want to buy today?" The question at the end of an evangelistic retelling of the gospel, on the other hand, is, "Wanna know more?" Gospel conversations become the means to gospel conversions.

Not monologues. *Dialogues.*

And as biblical illiteracy continues to proliferate in our modern culture, dialogue is becoming more important by the day.

The two of us live in an area of North Carolina known as the Research Triangle. It's one of the fastest-growing, more progressive metropolitan areas in America. Christians do still make up a sizable slice of the population, but the percentage of those who identify as believers continues to decline.

For this reason, our experiences with both Christians and non-Christians here have changed dramatically in the past two decades. Increasingly, the kind of conversations we have with people about Christianity require explaining to them what Christians really believe, in contrast to the way we're portrayed on TV or in the movies. We meet more and more people these days who both (1) are not Christians and (2) have few if any personal relationships with Christians. Obviously this leaves a lot of questions to answer, a lot of misunderstandings to correct.

And a lone, scripted presentation of the gospel just won't cut it.

But this is good news for Christians like you and like us, because learning a scripted evangelistic presentation that ends with a demand for response was always uncomfortable anyway. One of the reasons you probably freak out when you think about sharing Jesus with someone is because if you don't present a perfectly crafted plan of salvation, you're afraid of failure, or worse . . . you could accidentally send a person to hell—as if *you* are their savior, as if you're their only hope. Feeling put on the spot for getting the information right or else failing to see someone come to Christ has always seemed overwhelming.

But what if evangelism could look more like coffee with a friend? Or like sharing on social media? Or like hanging out together at a favorite lunch spot? What if evangelism could become simply another part of your day, part of your lifestyle of sharing Jesus?

Lifestyle evangelism is not really a *method* of evangelism. It's learning to casually communicate Christ within an ordinary life of gospel storytelling. For some, the idea of lifestyle evangelism has come to mean living a certain type of Christian life that might lead other people to ask about Jesus, merely by observing how a believer lives. This is not what we have in mind here. In this book, *lifestyle evangelism* means developing a lifestyle that enables *gospel conversations* to flow naturally through all the relationships we have

Because how much better would it be—think about it—to just relax and share Jesus naturally with people in normal conversations?

R-E-L-A-X

Starting a gospel conversation may sound hard, but it's not as hard as, say, hitting a Major League fastball.

People who know such things will tell you that hitting a baseball is the hardest thing to do in all of sports. Those who become good at it must learn to be adept at two seemingly opposite things: (1) waiting on the pitch and (2) being quick with the bat.

The pitcher, of course, is always trying to confuse the hitter. The ball may curve; it may sink; it may even appear to rise. Or it may just come at full, blazing speed directly over the heart of the plate. So, the hitter must first try to recognize the pitch, which means waiting until the last possible moment to swing. But then as soon as he commits, he needs to be quick with his bat, putting it squarely on the ball.

Wait . . . GO!

Not yet . . . SWING!

It happens so fast, it's nearly impossible.

But here's how the best coaches teach it. They tell hitters to relax—not because relaxing eliminates all the nerves a hitter may feel in the batter's box, but because a stressed mind is less focused. It makes you impatient, unobservant. It makes you rush things. *You swing too soon.* In the same way, tense muscles move slower. They're stiffer, more rigid. Less free, less fluid. They make you sluggish. *You swing too late.* Either way, you swing and miss.

Unless you're relaxed.

Great hitters learn to relax.

Confident players are relaxed players.

And the same thing is true for Christians who wish to communicate Christ more casually and naturally with others. Being relaxed helps you listen; being relaxed helps you know how and when to step in and engage.

Presentations lead to the opposite of staying relaxed. Presentations require preparation. Because as the presenter, you're the one who's supposed to have all the answers. The pressure is on YOU. So you can't relax before or during the presentation, only after. If then! Preparing for a presentation means focusing on the *presentation*.

Conversations, though, mean focusing on *people*.

One of us remembers a time when we were having dinner with our pastor and his wife. We ended up staying and visiting for quite a while, in no particular hurry, which meant we saw a lot of our waiter as he kept checking in on us. We didn't go there that night with the intention of forcing a gospel presentation on this person. But every time he came by the table, our running conversation with him kept picking up where it had left off.

We found out that he attended a local university, and this led us to ask about his area of study. From there we somehow started talking about philosophy and religious thinkers, which provided us an opening to talk about the difference between Jesus and other religious men. We didn't drive the flow of conversation there on purpose; we simply assumed God was involved in our interaction and would direct the topics as they came up.

Over the course of that evening, despite the conversation flowing in fits and starts, we actually ended up having quite a long discussion about the gospel, the sinfulness of humanity, and what it means to be in a right relationship with God. We would talk for a while until he was called away by another customer, then he'd keep coming back, wanting to continue the conversation. And finally, when we needed to leave, he asked if we could talk some more. We gave him our numbers and email addresses.

We didn't arrive at the gospel by worrying about the key points we'd wanted to make; we'd done it simply by keeping our attention on *him*, on the person. An ordinary conversation let that happen. At times we found ourselves jumping around and wandering off-topic, responding to his questions and the concerns he raised.

Not so, however, with a presentation. A presentation has a beginning, a middle, and an end. It has a predetermined path on which the presenter wants it to go. Before starting, he or she already knows the end. The presenter is the one in charge. In fact, if someone's presenting at a meeting and doesn't know what his or her next point is supposed to be—if the presenter just starts rambling and thinking out loud—that person may not be at the next meeting!

But a conversation has a starting place with *no* set end. When you enter into conversation with someone, you're unsure what direction it might take. You and a coworker may be talking about the weather over lunch and suddenly find yourself discussing the D-Day landing at Normandy. *What?* How'd you get *there?* Who cares! You're just hanging out with a friend.

That's probably why some people *prefer* that their evangelistic methods take the form of presentations, because it lets them be in control. Do you have a friend who insists on doing all the talking when you're together? Do you enjoy those conversations? Probably not. We all know *that guy* who always seems to be in presentation mode. When it's your turn to talk, you can tell he's not listening; he's only planning the next thing he's going to say. These are presentation people.

Conversations, on the other hand, are a shared journey on which the people involved collaborate to decide where the trip takes them. There's no hidden agenda, no surprise to be sprung on the other person around the next corner. In a conversation, the fellow travelers each take turns at the wheel. And even when they're driving, they may not always know where they're headed. They talk for a while, they listen for a while, and then they see where the journey leads.

So, just *do* this as your plan for evangelism. You most likely already do it anyway. You talk with people about your kids, your marriage, your job, your garden, your hobbies—all kinds of stuff. Good! Don't stop. Just remember, as with any drive across town, a conversation could always meet with a detour or change of direction that takes you another way.

Because when you're enjoying Christ and seeing his everyday impact on each area of your life, a conversation on any subject could instantly turn into a weightier discussion about having a relationship with God. You won't need to artificially steer it in a spiritual direction. Each conversation contains a spiritual dimension already. Your job is just to *r-e-l-a-x*! Because, trust us, you'll recognize when it's moving toward a spiritual moment. In fact, everyone in the conversation will know it.

Gospel Conversations: You Can Do This!

The reason ongoing, everyday conversations can't really keep from containing spiritual dimensions is because the gospel is not a Sunday-only topic. For one thing, Christianity is a way of life for you in addition to the way you worship. It influences how you treat people, how you interact, how you approach your daily life. You cannot NOT be a Christian. It's who you are. Everything is shaped by your faith. Therefore, it is natural for your faith to come out in how you talk, no matter what you're talking about.

The two of us, for instance, are both dads. And, no, we don't talk about parenthood in every conversation, but there's no escaping the fact that we see things, experience things, and think of things as fathers. So it hardly feels odd or unnatural, when we're in conversation with someone, to slip into talking about something related to being a dad. We are never NOT dads.

Something the other person says will remind us of a story involving one of our kids. And because being a dad is who we are, we'll talk about it. It's not like one of us left home that morning with our presentation ready for describing our daughter's latest sports injury (or whatever) and how we wanted to share it with someone. In the course of an ordinary conversation, the story just fit. So we talked about it.

The same can be true of your relationship with Christ. Your non-Christian friends will make statements to you in passing that open the door for spiritual conversation. Let's say you and a coworker are talking together about your boss, who you both know is unethical, condescending, and mean. Your coworker says something like, "He'll get payback one of these days for acting that way."

Even in jest, though, this person just made a theological statement. He or she may not possess a developed, thought-out, religious commitment to the principle of karma; but the statement itself gives you an indication of what your coworker believes about how actions, whether good or bad, relate to our future.

You now have a point of contact where the gospel tells a different story: a story about grace and forgiveness, about mercy and reconciliation; a story about bad people getting *good* things because of what God has done through Christ; a story about how he loves us enough to give all of us as sinners the salvation we don't deserve.

That's the kind of gospel conversation that can just happen naturally, and effectively, any day of the week, because you didn't limit the gospel to a presentation.

If you want to share Jesus without freaking out—if you want to be the type of person who can casually communicate Christ in ordinary conversation—but you feel the need to be prepared for it by thinking ahead, here's a suggestion: repurpose the time you could've spent rehearsing your evangelism speech and use it instead to evaluate your heart. Evaluate yourself in terms of what three characteristics people will quickly discern in you whenever you talk with them.

1. People can tell if you CARE about them.

Have you ever been talking with someone and sensed they really had no interest in what you were saying? You can see it in their body language; they're not really listening. You can hear it in their responses; their words are canned and insincere.

We've all known people, too, who call or come around only when they want something from us. We all know those who show partiality to the ones who can give them money or provide contacts or tickets to a ball game.

In the same way that you can readily spot this disregard in others, they can spot it in you. So don't give them reason to see it. Just make sure it's not there. Don't pretend to care about people. *Care about people!* Develop a genuine interest in others. Avoid thinking of your coworkers, neighbors, and acquaintances as mere cogs in the wheels of your life. Think of them as real people—people whom God made, people whom God loves. Treat people like individuals, not merely as extensions of yourself. Gospel conversations can build on that.

2. People can tell if you BELIEVE what you're talking about.

The apostle Paul warned his readers about people who were sharing Jesus from wrong motives (Phil 1:16–19). The best conversations grow from hearts whose motives are pure, who sincerely believe that this story of God reconciling the world through Jesus Christ is true—not just factually true, but true for *us*. True for *them*. True for everyone.

We don't show the truthfulness of the gospel by hiding our hurts and doubts. Instead, we show the reality of our faith by letting others see us trust Jesus when life is not perfect. The more openly involved you become with others, the harder you'll make it on yourself to maintain shallowness in your Christian faith. If you want to share Jesus with the people you encounter regularly, be constantly cultivating the kind of pure, godly motivations that genuine faith can provide you.

Even some pastors choose to remain a bit detached from church members, afraid the insincerity of their motives will peek through their conversations. Good guess why. Because . . . *they will!* Sincerity within solid relationships is one way to help with that. The more distant you typically stay from others, the easier it can be to fool them about the real depth of your belief in the gospel.

3. People can tell if you PRACTICE what you believe.

Some individuals are good at playing a role. Think of the excellent actors on television, in movies, or on the stage. Others are not so good. Think every fifth-grade theatrical performance you've ever seen. We can all tell the difference between good acting and bad acting.

And if you are acting as if your faith in Christ is of great importance to you, even though it's really not, people will eventually find out. They'll see it.

That's why it's actually a lot easier to make a canned gospel presentation to an anonymous person on the street than to have a gospel conversation with someone who really knows you, because the people close to you know well your weaknesses and failures. They know if your relationship with Christ has made you different. They know if you really *practice* your faith.

Notice we didn't say you need to be perfect, because that wouldn't be authentic either! But be the kind of Christian who responds rightly to your imperfections. Be the kind of Christian who truly lives out this faith you profess. All the evangelism books in the world won't help you if you're not practicing your belief in Christ every day.

When you genuinely *care* about people, when you truly *believe* what the gospel's all about, and when you're diligent and consistent in *practicing* your faith in Jesus, you will want to talk about him. And the people who live in relationship with you will want to listen.

And they'll want to know more.

{ CHAPTER 4 }

Evangelism Is Contextual

I have become all things to all people, so that I may by every possible means save some.

—1 Corinthians 9:22

Principle #4

Every context is an opportunity to share
the joy of the gospel with others.

Context is crucial. If you are in a movie theater and shout "Fire!", you are probably going to be in trouble. But if there really is a fire in the theater, you are going to be a hero. A song about misery is not appropriate at a wedding. When a friend's loved one is in the hospital may not be the best time to tell a joke about death and dying. Language is the same way. Words help convey a message because of the context in which they are used. Take the single word *plant*, for example.

- In the context of mechanical engineering, a *plant* is a facility designed for the manufacture of goods.

- To a biologist, a *plant* is a living organism that grows from the ground—like a green, leafy bush.
- When farmers hear the word *plant,* they think of getting their fields ready for seed, for planting season.
- A football coach, however, might use the word *plant* to tell a player how hard to hit the opponent. *Plant him!*

The context informs how you use the word. When you change from one context to another, the meaning of the word is different. If you were using the term *plant* within the context of farming, but your hearer thought you were talking about a facility for producing pharmaceuticals, things could get confusing very quickly. Evangelism is learning to get both parties in the same place, understanding language about the gospel in the same way, so that true communication can happen. By knowing your context, you can help your listeners know the gospel.

In Acts 2, as God dramatically filled the first New Testament-era followers of Christ with his Holy Spirit, he emboldened them to share the gospel with Jews who'd come to Jerusalem "from every nation under heaven" for the celebration of Pentecost (v. 5). Peter, seeking to explain the source of all this commotion, stood up to address the crowd, delivering a message centered around Old Testament prophecy. He claimed that Jesus of Nazareth—the one recently crucified and raised from the dead—was himself the promised Messiah. Three thousand people became Christians that day as a result.

Notice, though, Peter only needed to reference one passage from the Hebrew Bible (Ps 16:8–11) in order for most of his hearers to instantly know what he was suggesting, that Jesus is the true subject of that passage. No other explanation was really necessary. These were people who already knew the Word, who were familiar with it as part of their culture and practice. So Peter could say, in essence, "You remember that passage in the Bible? Of course you do. It's actually about Jesus, the man the Romans killed not long ago" (see vv. 22–24). Since

Peter and his listeners shared a common knowledge, he could employ this connection to share Jesus with them.

That was his *context* in Acts 2.

Several chapters later, however—Acts 17, in the scene from Athens that we've mentioned a couple of times before—Paul was in a different context entirely. He had wandered through the city marveling at the plethora of religious beliefs practiced there. Aware of its pagan culture, Paul knew he couldn't use the same approach as Peter did. If he'd said, "You know that passage in the Old Testament about a Jewish king?," they'd have had no idea what he was talking about. So, instead of starting with the Hebrew Bible, he told the gospel story from the beginning. He started with creation, moved to the spread of all nations and people groups across the earth, and then to the resurrection of Jesus, ending with the promise of believers' own resurrection from the dead.

Context.

It changes how we talk about things.

Imagine, for example, that you spent last Saturday night watching *Gone with the Wind* on Netflix. If on Monday morning you were sharing the story of your weekend with someone else, how would context determine the approach you took?

If you were talking to someone who is technologically inclined, you'd probably start out by saying, "I was watching an old movie on Netflix the other night." Because while they'd readily understand how you accessed the digital content, they'd be less likely to instantly picture in their minds the actors and scenery of *Gone with the Wind*. They might not ever have seen it.

If, however, you were telling it to someone a good bit older, you'd say, "I watched *Gone with the Wind* this weekend." Because they'd know exactly what the movie's about. But they might not know what all was involved in streaming it online. Context helps you know where to start in communicating so that you're sharing in a language that squares with the other person's experience.

And when you're sharing Jesus, you're always sharing him within a specific context.

You may be talking about him with someone who's primarily a *thinker,* a person who's motivated by facts; someone who's stimulated by deep, nuanced discussions.

Other people are primarily *doers,* motivated by action. They'd be most intrigued by those parts of the story that give them something to believe in, a cause worth living for.

Still others are primarily *feelers,* those who care deeply for others and are out front with their emotions. They need to know God loves them. They need to *feel* the gospel.

Yet even with all these contexts in mind, even with all the contexts that are out there—cultural, personal, spiritual, generational—the gospel still speaks to each person. And that's what makes sharing Jesus so exciting, so exhilarating. That's why there's no need to freak out. For though the context determines how you tell the content of the story, it never changes the content of the story itself.

Because, as Principle #4 says, *Every context is an opportunity to share the joy of the gospel with others.*

A Different Day

Some of us grew up in more of that Acts 2 world, where most everyone we knew went to church or at least identified with a particular Christian tradition. If asked, we'd say we were Baptist or Methodist or some other denominational stripe painted from the same broad brush. Most people had a pretty decent knowledge of what Christianity meant. Even if they chose to live contrary to the Bible, they at least knew what it basically taught and entailed.

So, during that time and place, Christians in the West had sort of a home-field advantage. Even people who didn't believe in Jesus had a general idea of the message, some awareness of who God is, and an understanding of right and wrong based at least loosely on Scripture. To be evangelistic in that kind of culture often meant (or still often means) convincing those who *think* they're Christians that maybe they're *not* Christians, not in the biblical meaning of the word, even if they go to church fairly regularly and put up all the appearances.

But this context is evaporating in North America. Even if the culture we've described here is in keeping with the type of community you knew growing up, chances are good you're reading this book today in a place where that world no longer exists—a place more akin to the Athens of Acts 17 than the Jerusalem of Acts 2. You're likely to live in a setting where your coworkers, friends, and neighbors form the majority of their core interpretations on life from a different starting place than the Bible.

So, we can't make the same assumptions about people we once did. If the average person entertains any thoughts about Christianity at all, they probably think of it in moralistic fashion. They think it means doing more good things than bad things. That's what sounds reasonable and logical to them in today's culture, in today's context. They may have an understanding of the gospel that is foreign to the Bible. Or they may not have an opinion of the gospel at all!

We ask you this, then: What's your first impression when you observe these attitudes and apathies taking such firm hold in the culture? When you consider evangelism in a context where people don't know that Jesus was born of a virgin, or lived a sinless life, or died a substitutionary death, or was raised from the dead for our salvation, what comes to mind?

Fear?

Some Christians, as they think and make comment on the current state of affairs, take an exclusively negative view on it. They see culture as dangerous, even demonic; as something the church needs to keep out, something to run away from and feel superior toward. But being aware of these cultural contexts is vital if we want to share Jesus with those who live within it. We need to see how culture

- represents the value system of our society;
- determines how people process information;
- influences how they think, interact, and communicate; and
- shapes the definition and expectations of "normal" behavior.

Your culture is your context. Not culture in the sense of large movements of humanity, but culture in the sense of the place you inhabit. If your children are in competitive cheer, or ballet, or travel sports, that is your context. If you are in a book club or practice cosplay, that is your context. Context is the place you live in and the people with whom you live that life. Your culture is the environment where the other people around you understand your language and speak that same language. To friends who share your hobby of painting, you don't have to explain the difference between acrylic and watercolor. Football fanatics understand touchdowns and screen passes.

As a Christian, you are in many different contexts. There is your church context where most people know and understand the gospel. And then, most relevant for this book, there are contexts where you almost always interact with non-Christians. Because you already understand your own culture, you can understand the language of that context.

To share the gospel with people in your context, you adjust your language to what they already know. Are you in a context where your friends know something about Jesus but simply haven't come to believe in him? Then your appeal is to their need for Jesus. Are you instead with people who have no clue what Christianity is about? Then you have to provide more information to them, and the journey to saving faith is longer.

You do not have to become a student of culture to practice the type of evangelism we are advocating. You already know the culture of your context because it is *yours*. We aren't asking you to become an expert on "American culture," but simply to recognize that your own culture provides clues for how to best share Jesus with your friends and neighbors.

Think about some of the contexts you inhabit, such as where you work, what you enjoy doing for leisure, or what your hobbies are. Now, what can you say about the people with whom you enjoy those activities? What are they thinking? What are they looking for out of life? What kinds of questions are they raising, and how does the gospel speak to those concerns?

Even more, can you identify ways to translate the gospel into the language of those contexts? Think about Peter and Paul in the passages above. Peter knew that his audience had traveled to Jerusalem for a great religious festival. He addressed their sincere and passionate desire to find salvation by showing them the message of the gospel from the Old Testament, their own Scripture. Paul knew that the people of Athens loved religious dialogue, so he engaged them with the story of Scripture, leading them to the saving gospel of Jesus through the open door his context gave him. Do your friends have religious or personal beliefs that might be an avenue to a gospel conversation? Like the Jewish people in Acts 2, are people in your life looking for hope and salvation? Or, like the Athenians in Acts 17, are they just interested in debating truth claims? Either way, you can find points of connection between the hopes and dreams of people in your own contexts and the life-altering truths of Scripture. Evangelism means learning to listen for cultural clues in your conversations with others to discern what elements of God's grand narrative they are most ready, most able, to hear and understand.

The Context You Embody

Each time you engage in conversation with someone, you are entering into a specific context that in certain ways is unique from all others. The person or people you're sharing with—whoever they are—are present with you right there, in that moment, and are nowhere else.

But not only do *they* and their own personal, cultural attitudes make the context unique. The interaction is unique (and ripe for the gospel) because of the context *you* bring to the table.

You are *who* you are, *where* you are, by God's design. On purpose. He has put you in this specific time and place—in your own specific context—so that he can use you to be a witness for Christ right where you're located.

Think of it. You could have been born a thousand years ago. In Tibet. Or Australia. And yet you weren't. (Well, not a thousand years ago anyway, even if you do actually come from Tibet or Australia.) You could have been born into a whole different stratum of society than the one your family occupied. You could have been born with brown eyes, green eyes, blue eyes, or no eyes. The point is, a lot of the things that distinguish your life from those of other people are personal details beyond your control that came together to make you unique:

- your parents,
- your body type,
- your ethnicity,
- your native tongue,
- your birthday, and
- your birth order,

as well as many other features about yourself and your placement in this world. And though perhaps you've wondered at times *why* you were born into your particular family, in your particular region of the world, in your particular generation, or with your particular temperament and makeup, they all mean something important in how you share Jesus. They give you a context that is unique to you.

As do your hopes, your dreams, your passions, and your interests. The things that bring you joy, the things that excite you, the things that fire your imagination, the things that can cause you to lose all track of time in pursuit of them—these inner drives are designed for more than just occasionally filling you with temporary happiness. Underneath it all, they serve as available vehicles God can use in helping you share Jesus with others.

Faithful lifestyle evangelism means seeing everything that makes you *who you are* as an avenue for the progress of the gospel. If you love art, for example, you're likely to be around people who love art. You speak their language; you understand their interests; you recognize their struggles. To you, it all may just seem like second nature, but your particular knowledge and interest puts you in relationship with people who would be hard-pressed to hear about their need for Jesus from someone like us. In fact, if either of us tried to engage in a conversation with somebody about the advantages and differences of contour or cross-contour drawing, they'd know in a moment we were out of our depth.

Introverts don't need to become extroverts to share Jesus. Geeks don't need to become jocks. Mechanics don't need to become medical doctors. All you need is to be yourself—confident, un-freaked out, sharing Jesus in the context of where you already live.

Do you hang out with other parents of small children? *Share Jesus there.* Do you work a blue-collar job? *Share Jesus there.* Are you a police officer, a paramedic, a physical therapist, a rare stamp collector? Share Jesus with the people where your life and loves have placed you.

Even your hard times can serve a similar purpose. You've most likely been through experiences in life that you would never have chosen, yet these circumstances present you with opportunities to help people hear the story of the gospel in ways that most others are not equally equipped to do. That's not the *only* reason you've been made to go through these challenges. We would never say, for instance, that God caused your dad to lose his job and move you to another city as a teenager just so you could use those unwanted lessons as instruments of evangelism. Nor would we say he gave you a certain kind of physical disease or emotional struggle simply so you could be there to share Jesus within those healing communities.

Rather, the more you see how God has uniquely wired and orchestrated your life, that's how much more you can learn to live for him (and talk with others about him) in the way he's created you to do it. Learning what you can and can't control about your life contributes to how you bear witness to the gospel of Jesus.

Greg Forster says it like this:

> You do get to decide how best to respond to the circumstances and conditions life presents you with, and that kind of personal liberty is a good thing. But you don't get to decide what the circumstances and conditions of your life will be, and those unchosen circumstances and conditions—including relationships and obligations—are a central part of who you are. To a large extent, they determine the scope and significance of choices that you will have the freedom to make.[1]

Only you can share Jesus exactly *where* you share him and *how* you share him. We cannot step into your context, assume your personality, populate our minds with your experiences and memories and background, and share Jesus with your friends the way *you* can share him. Only you can do that.

Such things create your context for being a Christian.

That's why a one-size-fits-all evangelism program is always less helpful than developing what we call "gospel fluency," a gospel intelligence. When you allow yourself room to speak about Jesus in a way that fits both your personality and your context, rooted in how God is forming and maturing you, your

---

[1] Forster, *Joy for the World*, 75–76 (see chap. 1, n. 2).

opportunities to share him will naturally increase in number, ease, and effectiveness. Simply by experiencing the grace of God in the circumstances of your life and recognizing how the gospel is working in your own personal context, you'll learn to retell the story so that others can see his gracious work happening in their lives as well. You'll establish ongoing, real-time patterns for sharing Jesus the way you were meant to do it.

You'll learn to leverage *everything* that God has purposed or allowed into your life, using your context for the advancement of the gospel.

Creating Context by Consistency

Your family, your physical characteristics, your personal predilections, your background and experiences—you can't really change any of these. Some not at all; some only slightly. Still, you do have real control over one certain element of your context: the consistency of your Christian lifestyle.

Whatever your context, being a faithful Christian witness means practicing an authentic Christian lifestyle. Not in the sense of injecting your culture with a Christian subculture, with a uniquely Christian lingo, dress, and practices. But in the sense of living in a way that others in the immediate context could say, "I don't know if all that stuff about Christ is true, but that person sure lives like they believe it to be true." The need to live a reliably Christian life within our everyday contexts cannot be overstated. If we don't live as if the gospel is believable, how can we ask other people to believe it?

Imagine the following scenario. Two moms—one a Christian, one not a Christian—each has a child who goes to the same school, and the mothers volunteer to plan a party for their children's class. When they get together for the first time to figure out what they're going to do, what do they talk about? They talk about the party! That's the context for their relationship. The Christian is not trying to leverage the meeting for a gospel presentation, as though her primary objective is to notch another witnessing encounter. They're just there to plan a party, and that's it.

But what if, in the process of planning the party, the Christian mom gossips about one or two of the other parents, is rude or unkind, and fails to complete the tasks she's agreed to cover? Is there much chance in the future that the non-Christian mom would ever be interested in hearing this Christian acquaintance tell her the story of Jesus? Very little.

If the Christian acts Christianly, however, and a friendship does evolve, these two parents will naturally have opportunities along the way to talk about their kids, their backgrounds, and their various experiences. An avenue may emerge for the Christian to both show and share the gospel of Jesus Christ.

So, it's no mere morality statement when the Bible says to "abstain from sinful desires" (1 Pet 2:11). For as the remainder of that verse from 1 Peter explains, these "sinful desires" that God frees us from in Christ literally "war against the soul." They fight against our genuine love for God and for other people. Though selfish desires appeal to our flesh—though they seem to be things we want or need to make us happy—they're actually harmful to us because they keep us from living inside God's good and pleasing will.

And since part of his will is that we share Jesus with others, our witness becomes one of the notable casualties whenever we fall victim to sinful desires. Sin dissuades us from talking about him. Sharing Jesus is only natural to us when we're faithfully, humbly walking with him.

More than drawing our attention away from God and other people, the cost of spiritual laxity—the cost of our hypocrisy—is that it dulls whatever witness we *do* try to give. That's why Peter went on in his letter to exhort followers of Christ to "conduct yourselves honorably among the Gentiles" (v. 12).

We live in full view of people who are not yet Christians. And an honorable life reflects the gospel of Jesus Christ. It allows unbelievers the opportunity to see God's grace in action as he gives strength and beauty to those of us who by nature are weak and unlovely. If we say that God has brought us out of darkness but we refuse to live as people enlightened, what do our lives say about God's power to save and transform?

As Jesus said, "Let your light shine before others, so that they may see your good works and give glory to your Father in heaven" (Matt 5:16). Doing so sets your life *in context* with the gospel. Because if you have one of those Jesus-fish stickers on your car, and yet you're often in the habit of being rude or impatient with others in traffic, well . . . you might be driving people away from Jesus rather than urging them closer. Bit of an overstatement maybe, but you know what we mean. The best way to inhibit our friends, family, and acquaintances from acknowledging the gospel story is to dishonor that story through selfish, unloving, prideful behavior.

By contrast, there's something confirming about the story of the gospel when we can show by our own conduct the natural results of believing it. As we live a life of humility, service, and love toward our fellow human beings, we point them to the intended outcome of the gospel: people in right relationship with God and with one another. In denying ourselves, taking up our crosses, and following Jesus (Luke 9:23), we validate the claims we make about Christ.

By his grace, we give our words a fitting context of character.

Context Comprehension

Every context is an opportunity to share the joy of the gospel with others. You don't have to go looking for opportunities for evangelism; those opportunities come along naturally as you live your life in ordinary contexts.

While missionaries are those who cross contextual boundaries for the purpose of sharing the gospel, evangelism as we are teaching it doesn't require that you learn a new language, embrace a new culture, or develop a new fashion sense. Faithfully practice and preach the gospel where you are already planning to go. Going to baseball practice with your son? Share the gospel in that context. Part of a Tuesday night bowling league? You're afforded opportunities for evangelism as you enjoy those friendships. Do you go to car shows or Comic-Con? Then bridge casual conversations about carburetors or comic books with the good news of God's work in Jesus Christ for the people in those contexts.

Open your eyes to every context you find yourself in. The context with your friends today—and with new friends tomorrow. The context when you are with coworkers who have failed marriages or financial disasters. The context when you meet a random stranger at a convention, or when you talk about hopes and dreams with your oldest friend. And every place in between.

There is a context you inhabit. It is created by who you are and where you have been. Each day you are with people you just get. You understand them. They are your context. You don't have to go to school to learn how to talk with them; you do it every day. Only now you must learn to talk with them about more than novel characters and batting averages. You can also have conversations about Jesus. In the context of work. In the context of play. In the context of your city, your town, your neighborhood.

You are a Christian with a story. Everywhere you go, you have that story. And if you'll listen closely to the people in your own context, you will see why God put you there. You will see how the gospel speaks to the people in that context and discover ways to help them hear that message.

{ CHAPTER 5 }

Evangelism Listens to the Needs of Others

Everyone should look out not only for his own interests, but also for the interests of others.

—Philippians 2:4

Principle #5

The issues people face are open doors to connect the gospel to them.

The theme of the previous chapter—about knowing your context—is really important because it reminds all of us we've never met a person or encountered a situation where the gospel doesn't work or isn't applicable. Plus, every one of us has been uniquely created and gifted by God to share Jesus effectively with certain people, in certain contexts, simply by virtue of who we are.

And now this chapter is a chance to go ultra-practical with it all, giving you some tools for helping you improve your gospel conversation skills. In *every* context.

You already have the ability. Our goal here is to instill your ability with confidence.

Speaking for myself (Scott), I am an admitted introvert. I spend a lot of time with people because of my ministry, but this usually drains my energy. In fact, believe it or not, I sometimes invent chores to do, like painting a room or working in the yard, just to give myself an excuse for being alone. So in order to be evangelistic in my lifestyle, I've needed to work a little harder on my conversation skills than a lot of people probably would.

One thing that's really helped me is trying not to overthink it. Not imagining the worst. Not caving to analysis paralysis. Not freaking out over how to transition a conversation toward the gospel. Just *listening* for where God is leading it.

A few of my students and I were in Dallas, Texas, a while back, where I was helping them do some door-to-door evangelism. I was mainly there to encourage and pray for them as they went around, but I could tell it wasn't going too well. They were struggling to maintain conversations with people and were starting to grow discouraged. Finally one of them came over and asked me what I thought they should do differently.

"Well, everyone and every interaction is unique. There is no silver bullet or magic formula," I told him. "The best thing to do is to spare yourself the pressure of getting each point in the right order, or making each statement perfect, or being sure not to forget anything. Instead, just listen. When you listen to what people are saying, the way forward will usually present itself."

Approaching the next house, we walked together toward a huge, tattooed man who was working on a car in his garage. My brave students froze at the street, so I stepped up and introduced myself. I told the man who we were and what we were doing. I invited him to a concert to be held the following night at a local church. Then I said, "Hey, one more thing I wanted to ask you before we leave. Has anyone ever talked with you about how you can have a relationship with Jesus that is real and personal?"

Again—please hear this—few people react angrily or aggressively to a question like that. They just don't. Most people respond quite similarly to how this gentleman did. He talked about his own church experience (he was brought up Catholic, he said) and told us that he wasn't really interested in religion.

Okay. That's fine. "Pleasure meeting you, sir."

See? No pressure. No drama. No trouble or hurt feelings.

We turned to walk away, just as a little girl came running past us and scurried into the garage. The man picked her up in his massive arms, and she gave him a cute little kiss on the cheek. Sweet moment.

"My daughter just had a little boy," I said, admiring this parental scene. "It's fun for me, watching her learning to be a parent. Fun but, yeah," I thought to say, "it's also really difficult to be a parent today, isn't it? Kind of scary actually, raising kids in this world."

This comment kept the conversation going. And after a few minutes of chatting along these lines—a subject which, of course, was close to the man's heart—I said, "You know, this is why I think a relationship with Jesus is so important. Life is too hard to try living it without help."

From that moment, the entire conversation changed. He asked me about how Jesus *could* help him be a better dad. He opened up about his sins and his past failures. We actually stayed there for nearly an hour talking back and forth with him about the gospel.

Was it because I'm such a pro at witnessing? Was it because I had my presentation down pat? Was it because I have a knack for being able to keep conversations alive without making them feel awkward for either myself or the other person? Nope.

It was because of Principle #5—*The issues people face are open doors to connect the gospel to them.*

Blessing and Brokenness

Take a moment to think about a specific conversation you shared recently with a coworker, a neighbor, or a friend. Not just a passing hello, but any conversation of substance. More than likely in the course of that exchange, part of what the person brought up as you talked involved one of two things: either (1) a place where they're experiencing *blessing,* or (2) a place where they're experiencing *brokenness.* These two topics provide the most natural foundation for discussing the gospel.

Over the next few days, listen carefully to what people are saying as you interact with them, and you'll see we're probably right. Whether in serious conversation or in casual chitchat, they will almost always share something related to a hope of theirs—a dream, a delight—or they'll raise a concern about something that's troubling them, something that reveals an area of brokenness.

Why does this matter? Because inside these areas of blessing or brokenness is where you can most easily, most naturally talk with them about Jesus.

Here, we'll show you what we mean.

A friend of ours was flying out of town recently and found himself seated next to a young woman who'd just placed a bag full of tennis racquets into the compartment above their heads. "So, you're a tennis player?" (*Duh.*) But, see, a conversation starts just that simply.

Yes, she was a tennis player, she said, after a quick laugh. She told him she was a freshman at a university in the Midwest, returning home from a tennis tournament in the Triangle. "Oh yeah? What school?" Turns out she was a communications major, focusing on the use of advanced technology. Her dream job, she said, would be to work for Pixar, the animated film company known for movies such as *Toy Story*. Tennis was her interest, but technology was her passion.

"And you?" she asked. "What do *you* do?" Our friend said he taught young adults like her about Jesus Christ. "Oh." (Admittedly, when we tell people we're professors, their eyes often glaze over and they put their headphones on.) In this case, she was interested in talking more.

She said she'd grown up attending church with her family but had lost focus on spiritual things after going to college. Lately, though, she'd been feeling a need, she said, a real desire to recalibrate her life around the faith she'd known as a younger girl. She'd sensed that she was missing something in her life, and the lack of it was causing her to long for what she'd lost.

Her blessing. Her brokenness.

Did you hear them?

Think back to what we've said in previous chapters. Notice there was no pre-scripted *presentation* happening here, just an ordinary *conversation*. Our friend didn't see this young woman as a project for him to fix, just as a person who happened to be seated next to him on an airplane. Yet because he was keyed into the kinds of things that people most often talk about in conversation, he was able to share with her a little of the gospel story and how it connected directly to her life.

He'd simply asked if she was a tennis player. She said yes. And by continuing to *listen*, he discovered the opening that let him naturally share Jesus with her.

You never need to force people to talk about the things they love. It's not a burden for them to tell you about their families, their jobs, and their various life interests. When someone is passionate about a hobby or something, they'll talk about it. For instance, you're never left to wonder if a person loves CrossFit or not. If they're into CrossFit, you'll know it!

The same is also true for the places where people are hurting, where they are experiencing brokenness in this world.

Dreads and worries will tend to find their way into everyday conversation because they're never completely out of mind. Just as the things and people that a person loves are right there on the tip of their tongue, the things and people who've hurt them are rarely far behind.

And either of these—all of these—are like open doors that you can enter with the gospel. The things people care about the most, just like the things that are causing them the most distress, are commonly the same avenues through which God is actively working to draw them close to him.

All they need is someone to help make the gospel a part of that existing conversation.

And why shouldn't that someone be you?

Conversation in a Digital World

By encouraging you to see how natural it can be to listen for conversations like these, we're not saying it's always easy. And part of the reason for this, which is more true today than ever, is that social media has created a culture unlike anything the world has ever known.

On the one hand, the hyper-connectivity we experience through Facebook, Instagram, Twitter, and even micro-stores like Etsy provides us with opportunities to communicate with people around the world, which is of course a great advantage for those of us who seek to witness for Christ. We live in a time when ideas can spread, when even a single voice can have significant influence. Yet on the flipside, technology has also created an isolated generation that increasingly struggles in social settings and, to a large degree, doesn't even really know how to have a meaningful conversation anymore.

In a *New York Times* article, psychologist Sherry Turkle, author of *Alone Together,* made several keen observations on the pervasive, painful reality of it:

In today's workplace young people who have grown up fearing conversation show up on the job wearing earphones. . . . We are together, but each of us is in our own bubble, furiously connected to keyboards and tiny touch screens. . . .

Texting and email and posting let us present the self we want to be. This means we can edit. And if we wish to, we can delete. Or retouch: the voice, the flesh, the face, the body.[1]

In other words, many of us have learned how to live around people without actually having to *be* around people. Through social media, a person can share parts of his or her life with hundreds (or thousands), and yet one of their greatest fears is being exposed. So they work hard to create carefully filtered images of themselves. And though they still desire deeper friendships and meaningful conversations, the technologies that connect them with others are systematically working against this desire, destroying the sense of real community they seek.

So in the face of these social challenges, we offer you five keys we've discovered that can help you consistently engage in healthy, gospel conversations.

1. Listen to the stories of others.

Everyone has a story. And one of the best ways to have meaningful conversations with people is to be listening for those stories, to pay deliberate and discerning attention to them. Because the truth is, each story is a micro version of the story of the Bible. The same elements that make up each individual's stories— failures, consequences, dreams, fears, the hope for a savior,

---

[1] Sherry Turkle, "The Flight From Conversation," *New York Times,* April 21, 2012, https://www.nytimes.com/2012/04/22 /opinion/sunday/the-flight-from-conversation.html.

and a whole lot more—are also included in the plotline of God's story. The gospel is good news because it intersects with these stories from people's lives. It meets them at their points of deepest need. It helps them celebrate their greatest joys and see them as gifts from a God who loves them and seeks relationship with them.

So as you meet people, as you talk to people, make sure you're purposefully listening for their stories. Those stories will show up in the midst of ordinary conversations—about family, hobbies, movies, books, sports teams, favorite places to take a date, sources of joy and sadness, and so on—but each will actually be providing you insight into where God is already working in people's lives and where you can be his ambassador (2 Cor 5:20), introducing them to our Savior.

2. Ask questions and listen for the answers.

Often as a believer, you'll find yourself in conversation with someone and you'll sense—you know what we're talking about—that you should say something about Jesus. One of the ways forward, instead of trying to come up with something to say, is to ask a question; not just to be asking it, but because you're genuinely interested in how they'd answer.

Too often when we ask someone a question, we stop listening almost as soon as they begin answering, and we start formulating a response in our heads. But what they're saying is what's most important, because what they're saying will give you insight into the person's spiritual condition and help you know where to go with the gospel story from there.

You see the power of asking questions in the account of Philip and the Ethiopian traveler in Acts 8. Philip could hear the man reading from Scripture, and Philip asked him, "Do you understand what you're reading?" (v. 30). This simple question allowed the Ethiopian to ask for help. Philip climbed into the chariot with him and led the man to faith in Jesus.

The context of a conversation in which you sense the Spirit leading you to talk about Christ provides opportunity to ask questions such as these:

- What is your faith background?
- When you attend church, where do you go?
- Has anyone ever talked with you about having a relationship with Jesus?
- Does the story of the Bible (the story of the gospel) make sense to you?
- Has anyone ever told you the story of the Bible and how your life fits into it?
- Would you like to learn more about what it really means to be a Christian?
- What reason would you give for not receiving God's gift of eternal life?

You can also frame questions around the biblical narrative itself, around those four big parts of the gospel story we've talked about.

1. CREATION: Have you ever wondered how things really got here? Have you ever thought about what makes something beautiful or ugly? Good or evil?
2. PROVISION: What makes you feel the happiest? What are the things you find the most satisfaction in? Why do you think they're even here for us to enjoy?
3. FALL: Have you ever tried figuring out why this world is in such a mess? What do you think causes all the evil and brokenness around us?
4. PROMISE: What do you think could be done to fix this broken world?

But again, you're not just asking questions; you're *listening*. Show people you truly care about them because you truly do! And keep enjoying your conversation with them.

3. Give genuine encouragement.

When people have questions about God, or when he's allowed events into their lives that are causing them to think about him more than usual, you want them to feel comfortable coming to you. But far too many unbelievers don't have positive relationships with Christians. They view us as joy killers. Judgmental. Negative.

Be sure you're actively working against that stereotype in your conversations with others, because there is no greater deterrent to lifestyle evangelism than Christians being mean or dismissive toward other people. You don't need to embrace a person's worldview or choices in order to be kind and encouraging to them. You treat them with dignity simply because they are someone God made, someone God loves, someone like you for whom Jesus died.

Jesus is our model here. Even a cursory reading of the Gospels paints a picture of him caring genuinely for others. He spent most of his time with people who'd been abandoned or neglected by contemporary society. He had dinner with prostitutes, tax collectors, and other "sinners," much to the disgust of religious leaders who asked his disciples why he would do such a thing (Luke 15:2). As Jesus traveled around, "when he saw the crowds, he felt compassion for them, because they were distressed and dejected, like sheep without a shepherd" (Matt 9:36). Rather than push people away, he desired to pull them closer to himself, no matter the depths of their sin. And we as his representatives today must remember that the Bible clearly tells us to "adopt the same attitude as that of Christ Jesus" (Phil 2:5).

Whenever you're talking with people, be kind to them. Encourage them. Show hope and patience. This attitude requires humility and selflessness.

We shared earlier in the book how we sometimes like to mess with those people who come by our houses, evangelizing for their various religious groups. But to be fair to ourselves and candid with you, hear us say we actually look to turn those visits into pleasant, engaging conversations. We let them talk freely about their faith, even as we share the gospel with them. We ask about their families, their studies, and their missionary work. We put our hands on their shoulders and pray with them. It's not uncommon for them to say, as they're turning to leave, "This has been one of the most encouraging conversations we've had in weeks," or even to ask if they can stop by and visit with us again sometime. And, of course, they're always welcome.

We never know if they'll hear the gospel with believing hearts. We hope so. But we do know their chances of putting trust in Christ are very slim if the only Christians they meet are rude to them. Be sure you're treating people well, with courtesy and kind attention. Our goal is simply to obey the golden rule: "Whatever you want others to do for you, do also the same for them" (Matt 7:12).

4. Speak to the heart as well as the mind.

One of the main reasons people don't share Jesus is the fear of being asked a question they don't know how to answer. But trust us on this: reaching people has less to do with how you deal with intellectual questions and more to do with how you touch their hearts.

Communicating the gospel is part science and part art. The *science* of evangelism is the unchanging truth of Jesus as revealed in the Scriptures. Facts and certainties are what speak to the mind. And that's definitely important, truly necessary. But the *art* of evangelism depends on the specific concerns and questions of the person you're talking with. Art speaks to the heart. And that's why some of the most effective evangelistic conversations feel more like counseling sessions than intellectual debates.

God created us—all of us—to be in a relationship with him that touches every area of our lives. As you share the gospel story, recognize its power is hardly limited to the factual and linear. Use it to communicate love, hope, and healing to the places where people seem to be needing it most.

5. Remember that the real person lives below the surface.

Whenever you're sharing Christ, be sure you're talking to the actual, living, breathing person in front of you, not to a stereotype. Few things end a conversation or destroy a relationship faster than assuming we know a person because of who they vote for, what they look like, or where they come from.

On September 11, 2001, one of us was living in a country where many people practiced Islam. As you can imagine, it was a strange time to be an American living outside the United States. Perhaps you recall the moods and feelings that seemed to prevail in those days, when many people were tending to lump all Muslims together and be suspicious of them, even those who had no connections to the radicals behind those attacks and rejected any form of Islamist terrorism.

We knew very few Muslims who weren't saddened and horrified by the attack. Many, some we didn't even know, went out of their way to show our family sympathy and compassion. Having lived through that experience, we learned how misleading and inaccurate many of our cultural stereotypes can often be. Putting people into a predetermined box, based solely on their background or beliefs, is not only unfair but inhibits your ability to communicate Christ to them.

People are people. We're parents, we're children, we're employees, we're friends. And we mostly all share the same concerns. We have fears about our future, guilt about our past, and are looking for something to help us get through life successfully and do something important with our time here.

If you want people to open up to you—if you want to be able to have conversations with them about Jesus—it will almost certainly require getting to know them. *Really* know them, not just a phantom caricature of them. And when you do get to know them, you will learn that many of your initial judgments were inaccurate or incomplete. You will discover a person who may even already recognize his or her need for Jesus.

Keep It Simple

It's amazing to see how naturally Jesus could transition common talk into spiritual conversation. One example is from John 4, where he turned a conversation about water into a discussion about spiritual life. You're probably quite familiar with this "woman at the well" episode, but read it with an eye toward how he truly listened to what the woman was saying and used it to speak to her heart.

> A woman of Samaria came to draw water.
>
> "Give me a drink," Jesus said to her, because his disciples had gone into town to buy food.
>
> "How is it that you, a Jew, ask for a drink from me, a Samaritan woman?" she asked him. For Jews do not associate with Samaritans.
>
> Jesus answered, "If you knew the gift of God, and who is saying to you, 'Give me a drink,' you would ask him, and he would give you living water."
>
> "Sir," said the woman, "you don't even have a bucket, and the well is deep. So where do you get this 'living water'? You aren't greater than our father Jacob, are you? He gave us the well and drank from it himself, as did his sons and livestock."
>
> Jesus said, "Everyone who drinks from this water will get thirsty again. But whoever drinks from the water that I will give him will never get thirsty again. In fact, the water I will give him will become a well of water springing up in him for eternal life."
>
> "Sir," the woman said to him, "give me this water so that I won't get thirsty and come here to draw water." (John 4:7–15)

Jesus was alone, waiting for his disciples to return with food, when he met this Samaritan woman near Jacob's well. He asked her for something to drink, a request that broke several cultural taboos. And the shock of it led her to ask him a series of questions about prejudice, nationalism, and worship styles, until eventually they were talking about God's plan for her life—God's plan for a woman who'd likely been wounded by society; God's plan for a woman who may have been the victim of domestic abuse, jostled from husband to husband, and who was currently living with a man who apparently refused to marry her.

Jesus took her question about the basic element of life—water—and leveraged it to talk about her most basic needs: hope and forgiveness. He started a conversation in her world and then turned the conversation into a message about the kingdom of God.

Beginning a conversation and turning it toward Jesus is easier than most people think. Because, as we've reminded you before, you've had hundreds of conversations in your lifetime in which you and another person transitioned from one topic to another seamlessly. Most casual conversations you have with friends involve more than one topic without confusion. So don't overthink it. Don't let your imagination run wild on you. Don't complicate the process and end up standing in your own way. You're just there listening. You're responding naturally.

You're letting areas of blessing and brokenness lead you to telling a story that you already know. People do it all the time. Without needing a rehearsed plan in their pockets.

Again, the problem with using evangelism tools is that they confine us. They tend only to work in limited contexts, under limited conditions. They keep us married to a method, which makes our conversations about Jesus come off sounding insincere and inauthentic. But the goal for evangelism, as we've said, is to develop a gospel fluency that naturally flows in and out of what we're thinking and saying. We don't merely apply his gospel to our lives; we apply our lives to his gospel. We step out of our own stories and step fully into God's.

As Christians, we always need to be training ourselves to see Jesus as the protagonist of this story we're living. He is the ultimate purpose and reason for everything that happens to us, every experience we have, everything we do. We see ourselves inside this real-life narrative where Jesus is our hero—where something has gone terribly wrong, and yet he's promised us a hope and a future that he alone makes possible by his death and resurrection.

You don't *need* a tool to be able to communicate this truth to others. Your genuine, personal walk with Christ each day will keep you experiencing the gospel every moment, will keep you preaching it to yourself all the time. It leaves you free then, when you're talking with others, to simply do what pastor and author Jonathan Dodson says: (1) *listen*, (2) *empathize,* and (3) *retell.*[2]

Listen. If you already know the person, you can ask about specifics. If not, you ask general questions. But you don't plan your answers. Show some respect and just listen.

Empathize. Non-Christians live non-Christian lives, which makes many of their stories and experiences uncomfortable for Christians. The language they use or the facts they include may cause you to blush. But fight the urge to judge or freak out. This isn't the time to try fixing all the problems they discuss but to listen compassionately. See if you can discern what God is doing in their lives.

Retell, meaning, retell their story redemptively. Give them a vision for what their life might look like in a relationship with Jesus. Empathize about the penalty and damage of sin and the brokenness of the world, but also offer insight into how Jesus handles the consequences and shame of sin.

---

[2] From a conversation with Jonathan Dodson, July 14, 2015.

Also, be sure to use any opportunity to tell your own story. How has Jesus met you at points of crisis and shame? How has your relationship with him given you hope and healing? Share your struggles and allow him to receive the glory for his grace in your life.

Many of the people you meet are open to a conversation about Jesus if you approach them with respect and a listening ear. Because, as we'll be highlighting in the next chapter, the gospel is good news for all people. Jesus died so that anyone who believes in him can have eternal life. Most people know their lives are not what they should be, and they're open to talking about what would make them complete.

Wouldn't you like to be involved in that conversation? You can be. You're made to be.

Anticipate a good experience, and just dive in.

CHAPTER 6

Evangelism Is an Announcement of Good News

This is why we constantly thank God, because when you received the word of God that you heard from us, you welcomed it not as a human message, but as it truly is, the word of God.
—1 Thessalonians 2:13

Principle #6

People are already interested in what is best
for them; the gospel is best for all people.

Throughout this book we've emphasized sharing Jesus naturally, sharing him casually, sharing him the way God created you to do it. We've talked about the importance of relationships, the importance of conversations; how evangelism is more about making friends than reaching prospects or making contacts. It's not a matter of closing a deal, as if you're selling a product to someone that they probably don't want or need.

Because of all this, there's really no reason for freaking out. Instead, you can just relax.

But that's not all. You can also share Jesus now with a new level of expectation. Because when you think of others as friends instead of as notches on your soul-winning belt, you start to assume that they'll be friendly back to you, that they'll be interested in your message. You're sharing good news with someone who's separated from their Creator, someone who's making all manner of life choices in a failed effort at filling the void. So you expect them to be open to the gospel, because you know you're speaking truth that reaches directly into their core needs.

It's as Principle #6 says: *People are already interested in what is best for them; the gospel is best for all people.* The change in expectation that comes along with accepting that statement will recalibrate your whole mindset.

One of us is thinking right now about the first time we ever tried sharing Jesus with someone who not only came from a different background but also spoke a different language. *Three* people actually. Three young men who grew up in a non-Christian context. And though by this point in my life I'd already shared Jesus many times, and had even taught many people to witness, I was struggling to communicate the gospel to these guys. Painfully so. I'd been trained to witness by using a plan of salvation that included several important catchphrases: (1) God's purpose, (2) our need, (3) God's plan, and (4) our response. Each of these four elements was vital to my presentation, and I wanted to get them right. But they were all in English, and they all assumed a knowledge about the Bible and about God that these men simply did not possess. And so the longer we talked, the more confused they became. I was having a hard time trying to say what I meant, feeling paralyzed by the need to get all my points across, to be perfect.

After several distressing minutes, I paused and said a quick, silent prayer: "God, you need to help me here. I can't do this.

I'm making things worse." Then, taking a deep breath, I said to the three men, "Let's start over. The Bible tells us that in the beginning, God created a perfect world, but because of our disobedience, we all became separated from him." Even with the language barrier, this straightforward retelling of the gospel story's first chapters led us into a much more natural, much less stressful conversation about sin, punishment, forgiveness . . . a conversation about Jesus. And by the end, all of them looked at me and said, "Okay, we're ready to believe."

Honestly, their response sort of caught me off guard, causing me to panic again. I remember thinking, *Wait, I'm not sure we've covered all the points properly!* But I decided to trust God's work in their lives, and the three of them received Jesus that day.

This experience taught me some valuable lessons:

1. God has called me to be his witness.
2. The gospel is his message.
3. The gospel is great news.

These biblical realities removed a significant amount of pressure for me. Because the truth is, sharing Jesus with others is meant to bring joy to our lives and glory to God. And when we share him from that kind of heart, *expecting* others to be as captivated by the gospel as we are, our joy will be contagious. People will see that what is good news for us can also be good news for them, that a relationship with Jesus is the very thing they're searching for.

New Life Where People Live

Think about what was behind Jesus's skill in talking about "living water" with the woman at the well, the story we told at the end of the previous chapter. He *knew* that what he was sharing with her could absolutely change her life. (As it did.) He was able to stand there in her world, as the woman tried to conceal her brokenness, and apply the gospel confidently to her heart.

She could do whatever she wanted with what he said, of course, but he could share the truth utterly convinced that it was the best news she'd hear all day.

You can do the same. Simply in normal conversation, you can enter the various contexts of life in which people exist, especially those contexts where you commonly live yourself, and feel certain that the gospel is their way of finding rest from their troubling questions. The gospel offers the satisfaction they're working so hard to seek.

Take the context of *your job*, for instance. The people you work with go to work to earn a living. Their greatest fears at work are losing their source of income, suffering a financial or professional setback, or the company going out of business. No one goes into business with a goal of failure or to declare bankruptcy. Men and women in business are, by and large, working to provide a living for their families and contribute to society. Unfortunately, many of them become consumed with success and discover firsthand the truth behind what the Bible says, that "the love of money is a root of all kinds of evil" (1 Tim 6:10).

Imagine the gospel getting hold of people's hearts and changing how they view their daily work. It would transform their lives! How might you share Jesus in that context? How can you make powerful statements to people in business about the relevance of the gospel, helping them see the wonderful message of Jesus Christ?

As you talk with your coworkers, you can show them that their desire for success and providing for their families actually speaks to who they are: people created in God's image, created for his purposes. Their desire to work and accomplish is a drive he placed inside of them as part of his gracious provision. It's not something that the gospel frowns on or minimizes but rather encourages and makes stronger, directing their work to even greater ends. It helps them see their business as a tool designed to serve people's needs, and how it can become a key platform for displaying God's goodness to others. It gives people's workdays a real mission.

You can also talk about the connection between business ethics and the teachings of the Bible, topics that naturally transition into conversations about fallen human nature, sin, and the need for healthy boundaries. Plus, anyone in business is painfully aware of the strain they feel in trying to balance their lives, the dog-eat-dog stresses of working to stay afloat in today's ultracompetitive work environment. The gospel certainly points out the kind of perspective and priorities that help us keep our work satisfying without overtaking our lives and identities. And your example as someone who's learned (and is of course still learning) this freedom that the gospel gives us can speak clearly to what we all really need and can experience.

The gospel communicates, additionally, to people within the context of *entertainment*. There are countless forms of entertainment that consume people's time and money. Whether streaming movies, attending concerts, watching sporting events, or visiting museums and art galleries, people love to be entertained. Those sources of entertainment can provide opportunities for sharing Jesus.

For example, we have friends who are geeks—they read comic books, play video games, binge-watch television shows, and even dress up as their favorite characters for the opening nights of movies or comic book events. People who participate in this form of entertainment don't really believe they are superheroes or movie characters; they do these things for entertainment value. They enjoy the camaraderie, the adventure, and using their creativity.

If you are a Christian who lives within this context and enjoys this form of entertainment, you are associating with people who need the gospel. As people desire creativity and adventure, the gospel speaks to these deep longings. Also, many of the story lines that make up these movies and books present both the hope as well as the danger of living in a fallen world. Take advantage of such opportunities to share Jesus with those in your context.

Other people find entertainment in mainstream movies or books. If you are a movie buff or you read novels voraciously, you have a natural context for evangelism. Join a book club with people who are not Christians. Do not demand that they read the latest Christian novel. Instead, read what everyone else is reading. But look for ways to connect the major themes in the novel, or the characters in it, to Christian themes. Look for ways to demonstrate that the greatest desires of the protagonist are universal desires that the gospel addresses. Leverage the questions that arise naturally from various sources of entertainment to bridge conversations to the good news of Jesus Christ. Arts and entertainment offer a ready-made context for evangelism.

Let's face it: people are more inclined to respond to stories that connect the gospel to their lives than to intellectual arguments that prove the veracity of a point. In fact, most people we know who reject the gospel do not do so for purely intellectual reasons. Plus, few people have become Christians solely because someone convinced them that statements about Christianity are true. Instead, people resonate with stories that impact their lives. The Bible is the single true narrative of God, God's work, and God's world. But evangelism is more than proving that the story is true. It is also preparing the hearts of hearers to receive that truth.

Deep within people's complicated lives, they're usually asking the same few, basic questions—questions such as these:

- Where did everything come from?
- What's gone wrong with this world, with my life?
- What can be done about all this mess?
- What does the future hold?

And can't all of these questions and the emotions they express find their ultimate answers in the living story of the gospel?

Another context is *sports and competition*. We live in a sports-obsessed culture. People stick team logos on their clothes, their cars, even on their houses. Kids' schedules (and their parents') are full of games, practices, and tournaments. And if that many people are choosing to invest so much time and energy into this one common area, it must be a place teeming with opportunities for evangelism. They're passionately engaged in looking for an experience that, while exciting in certain moments, is actually only hinting at the exhilarating joy they can find in Christ.

One of the things that sports-minded people value is winning, as well as the thrill of pulling for the underdog. The gospel gives you many ways of making related connections with them, of speaking to their innate love for a David and Goliath story.

Sports fans also have a high sense of justice, of right and wrong. (Witness the angry parent ragging the umpire from behind the backstop.) Competitive people can't stand to feel cheated; they demand that the official enforce the rules equally. But as someone who yourself stays immersed in the Bible story, notice how this instinct indicates people's readiness for listening to the gospel. After all, one of the core elements of the Christian message is justice being satisfied in Jesus.

You and your family might have friends you tailgate with on Saturdays in the fall. Hanging out in the parking lot of a football stadium eating wings and playing cornhole becomes a platform for helping your friends see that gospel. How? Tailgating is nothing more than enjoying community. People do not love to tailgate because they love to eat food in a parking lot. They tailgate because of the relationships it provides. They are seeking relationships. The gospel is about establishing relationships, both with God and with other people. That desire for relationships can serve as a foundation for evangelism.

Not only are Americans consumed with competitive athletics, but we place great value on our *health and fitness*. The fitness industry is a multibillion-dollar-per-year business built on our widespread desire for overcoming unhealthy lifestyles and achieving physical wellness. The inspirational talking points and techniques that the fitness industry uses to keep people driven and active borrows from the timeless story line of the Bible, especially in three ways: *uniqueness, community,* and *spirituality.*

Can't you just hear them?

"Each person is *unique.*" The makeup of our bodies and our individual health goals means there's no one-size-fits-all diet or exercise program. This truth should influence how we talk with people when they're telling us about their workout regimens. God has created every person as an individual, and the gospel speaks to how God values each one of us. When you share Jesus with someone, keep in mind that you're dealing with a unique, specific, one-of-a-kind person.

"There's value in *community.*" Gyms emphasize their memberships, and online fitness programs highlight their virtual communities. They all know a strong sense of community is crucial in increasing a person's potential for success, for sticking with their resolutions. And everyone who's tried and failed in the past is highly aware of this need as well. We are made for being in relationships. Community matters. And at a level much deeper than physical fitness, this basic human discovery shows how the gospel is such great news. Through Jesus we are adopted into the family of God. What's more, we're invited to connect with a local church, which serves as our primary hub for spiritual growth and maturing.

"*Spirituality* is important." No wonder the fitness movement keeps trotting out popular versions of yoga, meditation, and other inner-life ventures. Fitness professionals understand that spiritual health is one of the keys to physical health. Which is no surprise to us, right? Because it's the whole point of the Christian story. Our lives are much more than just the physical and material things we encounter. There is a spiritual, unseen reality that people encounter. People are often interested in spiritual matters. As people show interest in the spiritual or the invisible, there is an opening for evangelism. And as you share the gospel with those who are noticeably involved and influenced by this sports-and-wellness sphere, you'll know you're offering them an insight that can bring renewed life to their *entire* lives.

We could mention other spheres besides these three. Politics, for instance. Education. Science. Many others. But we think you can see how the questions and concerns raised in each of these provide openings for gospel conversations. And how the contexts themselves, the ones in which people operate, may in fact provide the connection from which the story of the Bible will best capture an individual's imagination.

You as a Christian—not just the preachers and the missionaries, but you as an individual believer—are called to live on mission directly within those spheres where God has placed you. And the message you've been given to share is not, as we too often convince ourselves, the last thing people might want you to talk about.

But a lot of them won't be attending church this Sunday. A lot of them won't be meeting and visiting with a professional minister anytime soon. But *you* are there, filled with the Holy Spirit and charged with sharing great, great news that would mean the world to them. Your sphere has become your mission field. And you should expect to find interested listeners inside of it.

Plus One

We hope that you, having read to this point, have begun enjoying even more fully the story of God's work for you. And we hope you're starting to brim with confidence in knowing that the gospel, when presented where people can understand it, is truly the means to their reconciliation with Christ. That's a good place for a Christian witness to be.

But it bears repeating (because the style of evangelism we're teaching may be new to you): evangelism is not only successful when someone prays and becomes a Christian. Neither does it demand that you ask for a decision about salvation at the end of each encounter. Instead, successful evangelism can be defined as sharing the gospel and leaving the ultimate results to God. You are effective in evangelism when you have a conversation through which you show how the gospel speaks to the questions and concerns of the person in front of you.

You want to ensure that the conversation moves from their present knowledge (or lack thereof) toward saving knowledge. Successful evangelism happens when we help the other person take at least one step closer to trusting Christ as Savior.

So you're more like the parent who, in playing a game of Ping-Pong or basketball with one of your younger kids, could finish them off with ease if you wanted. But what you value more than beating them is spending time with them, enjoying them, showing them things little by little that can help them grow in their knowledge and mastery and grasp of the game.

Casually communicating Christ, then, begins with meeting people right where they are. And this means recognizing that your non-Christian friends, coworkers, acquaintances, and so on have differing levels of knowledge about the gospel. Your goal is to keep the conversation moving so you can help the other person move closer to understanding their need for Jesus.

Some of these people grew up in Christian homes and may have a full awareness of what the gospel means. Others, though, who perhaps also grew up in a Christian family, completely misunderstand the story of God's work in Christ. Still others, of course, may possess a vague knowledge of Christianity without having ever really heard the genuine gospel, while some people won't know about Jesus Christ at all.

All this to say, there's a spectrum of knowledge about the gospel, and each person lies somewhere along it. Your task, in each evangelistic conversation, is to help move a person along that spectrum. You want to help take them to the place where they've obtained sufficient knowledge for making a reasonable choice of whether or not to believe the message.

Here's a visual:

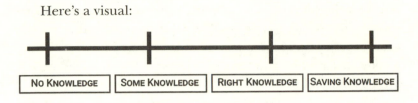

| No Knowledge | Some Knowledge | Right Knowledge | Saving Knowledge |

Notice that on one end of the line is "No Knowledge" of the gospel. These people may or may not know some limited information about Jesus or Christianity, but they don't know the gospel as God's saving message. Non-Christians at this stage can't express a real opinion about the gospel even if they offer opinions about Christians or Christianity. Their understanding is so far from accurate that they really can't be said to have *rejected* Christianity; they have never really heard its core message. Obviously, there are unreached people groups in the world who live at this far end of the spectrum, who don't know the first detail about Christ. But—just as tragically—there are people in your life and your surroundings right now who, even if they've heard of Jesus, have not heard about the Jesus of the Bible.

At the other end, of course, is "Saving Knowledge" of the gospel. But we're not speaking of a person who knows enough to be able to affirm the veracity of the biblical story. We mean someone who possesses a knowledge sufficient for salvation. According to Romans 10, a person cannot be saved unless someone shares, and unless the hearer receives knowledge of the genuine gospel. So, getting someone to this point is the goal of evangelism. We can't control whether they receive the gospel message, but we can control whether or not they hear it.

Okay, so in between these two extremes are points of increased knowledge and understanding, as indicated by the hash marks we've added. Begin thinking of evangelism as telling the gospel story in such a way that people can move along that line, one step at a time, until they reach a full, saving knowledge of the gospel.

We call this the principle of "plus one." In each gospel conversation, embrace the goal of wanting to help that person grow one step closer to a saving knowledge of Jesus than that person was at when you started. There's a lot less freaking out involved in that.

Your responsibility is not to convince people to become Christians, but simply to make sure you've given them enough to make an informed decision. As we've said before, you don't need to prove the Bible is true; you only need to explain the gospel you already know to be true.

That's what is best for them, whether they know it for themselves yet or not. So you can allow yourself to relax, listening for where their knowledge currently stands, and then helping them (through conversation, remember, not through monologue) to get "plus one" nearer to the relationship God desires for them. For *all* people.

Barriers to Belief

If we were to give a title to this spectrum we've just described, we could say it's "*How* People Become Christians." In other words, as people hear the message of the gospel, they move toward actually placing their faith in Jesus Christ for salvation. But while there is limited (or no) understanding of the gospel or an inaccurate understanding of the gospel, there can be no conversion. Evangelism is helping people move along that path toward becoming a Christian. But we'd also like for you to imagine another important spectrum to keep in mind as you're sharing Jesus: "*Why* People Become Christians." Because as an evangelist, you not only need to try discerning *what* people know about being a Christian but *why* they're not Christians.

Think of the line we introduced earlier. The two end-points are similar; this time, you could label one end "No Understanding." In other words, the person is not a Christian because this person *does not* understand the gospel message.

On the other end of the spectrum would be "Conversion." In other words, the person has become a Christian. In between these opposite poles, place "Ignorance" of the gospel and "Acceptance" of the gospel.

Here are four reasons the person you are witnessing to has not yet become a Christian. As you share with that person, you will want to recognize *why* they have not received the message.

1. Hostility

Some people have been hurt by Christians or by churches, to the point of calling the treatment they've endured abusive. And in far too many cases, of course, the abuse has been terribly real—spiritual abuse, psychological abuse, even physical or sexual abuse, all at the hands of people who claimed to believe the gospel and follow Jesus. These hurting individuals may have a correct understanding of the gospel, but trying to deal with the pain they've been through has left them hostile to it.

Other people are hostile to Christianity because of cultural biases, having come from parts of the world where they were taught to believe that Christians have caused great harm to their people and are continuing to do so. Nevertheless, the gospel is still what they need—it's what *all* people need—and we must be willing to have conversations with those who are hostile to Christianity, listening to their stories and sharing what we know to be true.

2. Suffering

Non-Christians may also reject the gospel because of the suffering they've seen or experienced in the world. The problem of evil is a real barrier to some people. Even if they know the gospel's explanation of evil as being the consequence of sin and not the will of God for his people, they still find the presence of evil and suffering a deterrent to Christian belief. More than once we've heard people say, "I cannot believe there's a God when I see all the suffering in this world."

This is a tough one, because there's really no explanation sufficient enough to help some people understand why God allows certain kinds of suffering. But the gospel does give a solution to that suffering, and receiving Christ as Lord can help a person make peace with it.

Tell the story, both with your words and especially with your life. Consider this: perhaps your own participation in people's suffering, as you empathize and sympathize with them, can be a way they hear the gospel with their eyes. Additionally, you can continue to highlight that part of the story where God joins us in our suffering through the incarnation of Jesus, sharing in the sorrow of our lives so that we can know the good of his life. By meeting people in their suffering, treating them with genuine care and concern, you become more able to communicate the good news in the midst of our shared pain and discomfort.

3. Refusal

Some people who know the gospel fairly well still prefer to worship another god or follow another religion. They're not openly hostile to Christianity; they've simply refused it. They've chosen to embrace and live by a different story than the gospel. They understand what you're saying about Jesus; they just don't believe it to be true.

Of course you can't *make* them believe it. But you can always keep making the gospel part of your conversation. And you can demonstrate through your life that this story that means so much to you is worth their belief as well. Faithful Christian living demonstrates to your hearers that you are thoroughly convinced the gospel has immense value. Let them see in you an unwavering allegiance to the message you share with them.

Though they may continue to reject the gospel, be willing to respect their decision and remain friends with them. Because as long as you maintain a relationship with someone, even with people of other religious persuasions, they'll be happy to listen to your story as much as you're happy to listen to theirs. The friendship doesn't end just because they refuse to trust Christ. The friendship is what keeps the lines of communication open for you to keep your message persistently consistent.

4. Apathy

Some people are simply apathetic toward the gospel. In fact, we'd daresay most of the people with whom we share the gospel fit into this category. They don't really give much thought to becoming Christians. They're working hard to pay their mortgages, keep their kids in school, finish their work projects, get promoted, help a son with his algebra homework, make it to a daughter's softball game on time, find a spouse, save money for a new home, or whatever activities occupy their lives. It's just all a full-time job. And it would still be a full-time job whether or not they were a Christian, so Christianity simply doesn't factor into their daily lives.

In many cases such people are relatively happy, healthy, and well-adjusted, and aren't searching for the meaning of life on a regular basis or for a solution to their deepest needs. They may possibly be open to the gospel, though of course they'd prefer it on their own terms. For instance, they'd like to keep their Sundays as great days for sleeping late and resting up for the week ahead. And barring a major crisis in life, which they probably haven't encountered yet, they're just a little unclear what they really need the gospel for. Plus, a lot of the Christians they know aren't all that "Christian," if you know what we mean.

So whereas those who are hostile to Christianity make a conscious decision to completely reject the gospel, or perhaps even work to dissuade others from it, most people just don't see how it relates to their current situation. Yet too often, we as believers have played right into how they feel because we've not offered them opportunity for trusting Christ. They've not had someone show them that the gospel is not only a story of what God did *for* them—Jesus's life, death, burial, and resurrection—but is actually a story of what he desires to do *in* them.

The gospel is not merely a message about how to "get saved." The gospel is the story of God's desire for relationship with people. The gospel is a story of love, and *love involves relationship.* Jesus didn't die so people could go to a place like Disney World. He died so they could know him and be known by him, to be fully known and fully accepted. And spend eternity with him in heaven.

When you share Jesus with people who are apathetic about Christianity, you're not primarily telling them how to get to heaven or how to get all their problems solved, even their deep sin problem. You're sharing with them what God has done so that they can be rightly related to him. You're loving them enough that, because they're your friend, you want to introduce them to your kind and gracious God, Jesus Christ, who wants to live in intimate fellowship with them. Because he loves them.

So, whether hostile or confused or disillusioned or defiant or simply disinterested at the moment, everyone has their reason for keeping their distance from the gospel right now. But the closer you draw to people, and the better you know them, the more confident you'll become that your story is just too good not to get through to whatever their "why" happens to be.

Open Season

In his book *Fools Talk: Recovering the Art of Christian Persuasion,* Os Guinness writes, "Our age is quite simply the greatest opportunity for Christian witness since the time of Jesus and the apostles, and our response should be to seize the opportunity with bold and imaginative enterprise."[1] Gone are the days

---

[1] Os Guinness, *Fool's Talk: Recovering the Art of Christian Persuasion* (Downers Grove, IL: InterVarsity Press, 2015), 17.

when social pressure and morality could serve as an apparent substitute for faith. People have made their life choices, and at some level they're suffering under the consequences of sin. Therefore, we're living in a culture that is seeking what the gospel promises. The times are ripe for Christian witness, and we dare not shrink back.

But they're not asking for that witness to be a genius or to be able to discuss deep philosophical issues. Most people are looking for someone who cares about them as a person, as well as someone whose life and words match each other.

Of course, Bible knowledge is helpful, but when you can talk comfortably about Jesus and about the difference he's made in your life, you can count on people wanting to listen. The world is so broken today, and the culture so desperate, that more and more people are open to having spiritual conversations. You might not have all the answers, but you can be like the man in John 9 who said, "One thing I do know: I was blind, and now I can see!" (v. 25).

CHAPTER 7

Evangelism Is Best in Relationships

In your hearts regard Christ the Lord as holy, ready at any time to give a defense to anyone who asks you for a reason for the hope that is in you. Yet do this with gentleness and respect, keeping a clear conscience.

—1 Peter 3:15–16

Principle #7

Gospel conversations must be grounded in relationships, both with Jesus and with others.

Let's be honest. One of the greatest hindrances to sharing Jesus is that most of us don't know enough people who don't know Jesus.

Too many of us live inside Christian bubbles, tucked inside the Christian subculture. We have only Christian friends, Christian family members, maybe even mostly Christian coworkers. We go to movies with Christians, have parties with

Christians, and spend the majority of our discretionary time almost exclusively with Christians. We do church activities with church people doing church things, because church friends are our real friends, and because church activities are what they tell us we're supposed to be doing. Everyone else is just a distraction to that, as if they're so much background noise.

But all this Christian busyness leaves us little time for building relationships that are true and genuine with people who are not Christians. As a result, the people with whom we need to be sharing Jesus become impersonal subjects to us, meaning the evangelistic methods we try using with them are impersonal as well. We share the gospel (if we share it at all) and then leave, never to interact with them again, because there's not an ongoing relationship to come back and revisit.

And this is a real problem.

Too many of us as Christians have become so insulated from the rest of society that we no longer have the opportunities nor the skill set to share Christ winsomely with those who aren't in our church circles. We've mastered the luxury of fellowship with the saints, even as we claim to want to be like Jesus, though his lifestyle caused him to be known as a friend of sinners (Luke 7:34).

We walk around with a gospel message about the most meaningful relationship of all. And perhaps one of the main reasons we freak out when we think about sharing it is because we don't have the relationships to swing it—the kinds of relationships where sharing Jesus could actually, finally, come naturally.

It brings us to Principle #7: *Gospel conversations must be grounded in relationships, both with Jesus and with others.*

Sharing with Those You Know

While it's true that many Christians don't have enough relationships with unbelievers, the fact is this: most of us are actually more connected than we think we are. Let's go through a little exercise together that will help you see the people around you through gospel-sharing eyes.

Grab a pen, and get ready to write down some names.

The following chart is adapted from W. Oscar Thompson's classic book *Concentric Circles of Concern*.[1]

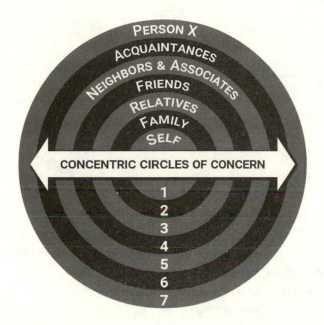

The process it takes readers through was originally designed as a guide to intercessory prayer, but it's mainly a good way for Christians to identify the different relationships they have. For our purposes in this book, you can use it as a way of thinking about the spiritual condition of the people you name.

We'll walk through it one ring at a time.

First, think about your *immediate family* (people you see often), as well as your *extended family*, your relatives (people you

---

[1] W. Oscar Thompson Jr. with Carolyn Thompson Ritzmann, *Concentric Circles of Concern: From Self to Others through Life-Style Evangelism*, rev. ed. (Nashville: B&H, 1999).

may see only occasionally). Are any of them unbelievers? If so, or if you aren't sure, jot their names down.

Second, what about your *friends*? Do you have any friends who are not believers? Probably not all your friends are fellow Christians or church members. Include Facebook friends in this too, if they're people with whom you communicate fairly often. Add their names to your list.

Third, who are your *neighbors*? Think about coworkers, classmates, your kids' classmates and their parents, sports friends, and the like, including—of course—the people who live on your street or in your building. Think about the people you spend time with socially. Maybe you don't know everything about them, but you know their names and something about their families. Ask yourself how many of them know you're a Christian. And how many do you know are Christians themselves? Add the rest to your list.

By the way, in thinking about neighbors, a friend of ours did an informal survey among a crowd of Christians. He asked how many of them had grown up in a Christian family. Then he asked those who'd raised their hands, "How many of your families ever talked about reaching your unsaved neighbors for Christ?" By his own estimate, having asked this question several times in several different settings, fewer than 10 percent of Christian families ever talk about or try to reach out to share Jesus with their neighbors.

Fourth, as the circle expands, think about *acquaintances,* those you know by name. Maybe you see them only now and then, primarily in settings that do not foster personal relationships. Think about banks, gyms, grocery stores, and so forth. Look again at your list of Facebook friends or at the contacts in your cell phone. Can you find five people in there with whom you'd say you have enough of a relationship that you could invite them out to coffee or to an online chat and they'd likely accept? Add those five names to your list.

Then finally, the last domain is *Person X*. This is someone you don't know but you may encounter along the way. It could be someone on an airplane, in a restaurant, or a person who engages you via social media. It could be anyone, really.

One of us remembers a time when somebody dialed our number by mistake. I could tell the person was distressed about more than just misdialing, and I asked her if she was okay. Turns out, she was trying to reach a relative to tell them about a death in her family. I told her I was a Christian, and asked if she'd like me to pray for her. She seemed touched by that, as most people are, and it opened up an opportunity to talk with her over the phone about Jesus and about the hope he gives us in Christ, even in the face of death.

Some people, of course, get really nervous when they think of talking with strangers about Jesus. Maybe you'd put yourself in that camp as well. But we want to propose that this *Person X* figure represents "The Power of X." Students tell us this has been one of the most helpful concepts for evangelism we've ever taught.

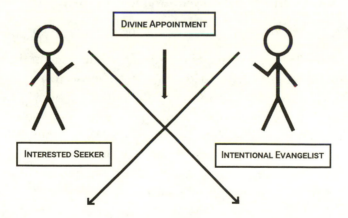

In the opening chapter of this book, we encouraged you to pray daily for opportunities to share Jesus with others: "God, I know you love people. Give me an opportunity to help someone today see your love for them and hear of how they can enjoy your work in Jesus Christ. Give me the boldness to talk with them about Jesus."

Remember that? If you've been praying this prayer, you should expect God to be leading *Interested Seekers* to you. You're living your life with a heart turned toward him; you're asking for evangelistic encounters; and God, in his sovereignty, will allow you to cross paths with people who are interested in talking with you about the Savior.

When you encounter someone—*Person X*—this is what we often call a "divine appointment." Everything else about your normal life changes, and you join God in his work of letting you introduce him to that person.

How can you identify a divine appointment? Is there any way to know if this conversation you're having is indeed ordered by God? Yes, we think so. Over the years we've discovered three questions you can quickly ask yourself. If the answer to any one of them is yes, you should probably start paying attention for ways to transition the conversation toward the gospel.

1. Is the person talking to me about spiritual things, about God?

Romans 3 contains some of the strongest language in the Bible, confirming that sinful people do not choose to pursue God unless he is already working in their lives. "There is no one righteous, not even one. There is no one who understands; there is no one who seeks God" (vv. 10–11). So when someone starts asking you questions about religion or spiritual matters, you can assume that God is the one who's been opening their mind to what the gospel offers them.

Maybe the person is talking specifically with you about God. Perhaps they're questioning his presence or his goodness in the face of a disaster or serious illness. Maybe the conversation shifts to church or a religious event. Any of these could be a signal that something in their mind has been awakened to God.

But don't limit what their questions or statements need to be. Some people don't really have a category for God, but the ideas they're bringing up with you do orbit around the spiritual world or another religion. Perhaps they say something about Islam or about how meditation has helped them. Maybe they talk about peace or hope or joy or another type of spiritual idea. Any of this "God talk" could be an indicator that God is at work.

2. Is the person talking to me about a problem so significant that they cannot find a solution on their own?

Most people are self-starters and prefer to work things out on their own. In addition, people typically like to stay private about the problems they're facing. So when an unbeliever begins talking with you about an issue big enough in their life that they feel the need to seek help, even to the point of talking about it with a mere stranger or acquaintance, it may be God getting their attention.

Consider this: of all the people on the planet with whom this person could be talking, they've chosen to talk with you—someone who's specifically been praying for God to send people your way who need him. By exposing these areas of brokenness to you, this person is essentially saying, "My life is not okay. Do you have any answers for me?"

One word of warning, however. When someone shares a problem with you, resist the temptation to become a pop psychologist rather than an evangelist. Point to Jesus and the power of the gospel rather than promoting solutions you've learned from books you've read, podcasts you've heard, or other tactics you may have tried yourself. When God places a distressed, discouraged person within your proximity, your job is simply to share Jesus with them.

3. Is the person expressing interest in my life in areas that are affected by my relationship with Christ?

No matter who you are or how ordinary you consider yourself, God has done a mighty work in your life. He's forgiven your sins; he's given you hope for the future; he's transformed elements of your behavior, attitudes, relationships, and more. You are a "new creation," the Scripture says (2 Cor 5:17), and it shows.

Maybe, for instance, someone's noticed something unique about the way you parent, and they've gone out of their way to mention it to you. Maybe they've said they admire the strength of your marriage, or your humble patience in a tense work setting, or your ability to be forgiving toward someone who's been unfair and unreasonable with you.

You recognize, of course—knowing yourself the way you do—that God has had to do a lot of work in your heart to bring your selfishness or stubbornness under control. You know better than anyone else that whatever character and perseverance you display is completely dependent on Jesus.

But here's something else that's good to know. A big reason that he brings about these developments in your heart is to gain glory for himself, to reveal how he pours out his grace on naturally sinful people. So someone's sudden interest in one of these areas from your life is an invitation for you to declare how God's power is what does it, and how the power of his gospel can accomplish the same kinds of things in this other person's life as well.

Can you think of a recent encounter with someone in which you could've said yes to any of these three questions?

These clues don't guarantee that your conversation with someone will result in that person's immediate conversion to Christ. But from our experience, they do indicate that God is at work in the situation. And when he confirms he's already behind a divine appointment, you can walk directly toward it without the least hint of freaking out.

Mission Central

From *Person X*, let's look back to those relationships that exist in the inner circles—the family members and friends who are closest to you. If you're like most people, the idea of talking with these folks about Jesus is perhaps the most nerve-racking of all because, like we've said before, they're the ones who've seen you on your worst days.

Yet since they operate at such close range to you, these are actually the relationships where the power of your changed life can echo the loudest. They're the people with whom you can often do your best job at evangelism without long, detailed explanations.

The following graphic illustrates this truth.

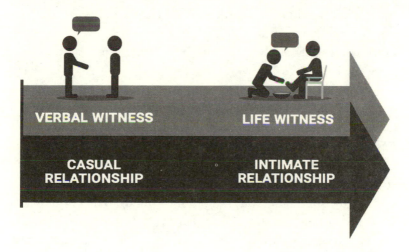

The more intimate a relationship, the less often you need to speak about Jesus with that person and the more you can depend on your own actions to be your testimony. Try using more of this approach when you think about how best to share the gospel with people you see on a routine basis.

But the more casual a relationship, the inverse is true. As the picture illustrates, verbalizing your faith early is essential in these types of relationships. Then, the longer your relationship continues with that person, and the closer they become to you—moving from acquaintance to friend—the more your lifestyle of character and compassion can serve as the most frequent witness of your faith.

Here's why we bring this up. Many Christians mistakenly assume that in the early days of a relationship they need to earn the right to speak about Christ. So they remain relatively silent about their faith. Experience proves, however, that the longer you wait to introduce him into a new relationship, the less likely you'll ever be to do it. At some point it becomes too awkward to bring up, and you start praying for somebody else to tell them about Jesus.

Once you've shared your faith with someone, once the person knows where you stand, it's no longer necessary to turn every conversation into a witnessing event. You can begin to more commonly allow your changed life to serve as the platform for your words.

We heard of a student from our seminary who developed his own strategy along these lines, trying to bring a more deliberate balance between his life example and his verbal witness. Rather than struggle to make every conversation with his coworkers contain the gospel somehow, he landed on what he called "the practice of five." He decided that in roughly every fifth conversation, he would say something to them about Jesus.

The number may be different for you. In fact, there may be some relationships where you would want to speak intentionally about the gospel more often. Either way, we think his is a great strategy. The beauty of it is how it creates an intentional process for casually communicating Christ with those close to you, yet without becoming overbearing and preachy.

We all want to maintain good relationships with our non-Christian friends, family, and coworkers. We don't want the neighbors running inside whenever they see us come home. Treating evangelism like telemarketing is a terrible way to

maintain friendships. Do you know someone who's always trying to sell you insurance or essential oils or some other commissioned product? What do you do? You unfollow or mute
them on social media; you ignore their phone calls; you avoid
them in the breakroom. Why? Because you feel like a target,
not a person. And no one wants to be somebody else's target.

Be sure to avoid even the appearance of being interested
in someone solely because you see them as a mark for your
evangelistic prowess. Genuine conversations are what build
relationships.

And relationships are the best place for evangelism.

Again, it's *lifestyle* evangelism. You don't set out with a plan
to "get someone saved." You don't head to work on a mission
to see all your coworkers come to Christ by Christmastime. You
just . . . go to work. Be yourself. Be the genuine Christian you
already are. You pursue a lifestyle that presents opportunities
for conversations about the gospel.

It's sort of like how you handle new fish when you buy
them at the pet store. If you fill the aquarium with tap water
from your house and then plop the fish directly into it, they'll
die from the shock. Instead, you bring them home in a bag
containing the water they've already been accustomed to living
in. Then you submerge that bag into the new water, and after
a period of acclimation, the fish feel comfortable swimming in
the water you've provided.

In lifestyle evangelism, as you let people know about your
faith and the difference it makes in your life, you get to know
them; they get to know you and the power in your life. You talk
about Jesus, sure, but also about each other's kids, vacations,
friends, family. One day you might find yourself talking to
them about art or music or the headlines or video games. But
whatever you're discussing, you are deepening your friendship.

And yet you're always aware that during these conversations, in the middle of these relationships, opportunities to
retell the story of the gospel (or whatever parts of the story

fit into that day's conversation) will naturally appear, simply because your friends know you're a Christian. Somewhere in those conversations, Jesus will become front and center.

That's because, while sharing Jesus is casual, it's also intentional. Not artificially manipulated, but vital. Whereas the everyday stories you tell to friends speak of things that are personal to your *own* life, the gospel story has tremendous bearing on *their* lives too. On everyone you know. And in every possible way. Not only is everyone, as a fellow descendant of Adam and Eve (what's known as the *external* extent of the gospel), impacted by the story of Scripture, but every single aspect of their individual experience is touched by it as well (the *internal* extent of the gospel). Every person on earth is involved in it and can receive the promised salvation that God offers through faith in Jesus.

The reason people at soccer practice listen to you share how things are going at your work or in your family is because they're interested in *you*. But the reason they need to hear the story of the gospel is because it is of ultimate interest to *them*. The gospel is not a private, personal matter between you and God. Sharing Jesus means telling the story of what God has done on behalf of *all* people . . . you *and* them. The gospel is the story of God doing something good for them.

You don't share Jesus just to make conversation with people; you share him for a reason. You tell others the gospel because you think, not only *should* you receive Christ, but I really *want* you to receive him.

You evangelize because you want other people to have a relationship with Jesus Christ.

Questions among Friends

No matter how winsome or prepared you are, you'll sometimes be asked questions that you feel unprepared to answer. This is normal. After all, you're introducing new ideas to someone. You are asking a person to make radical changes. If they're not asking questions, that's probably a great sign that they are not really considering the implications of the gospel.

However, there's no reason why anything they might ask should paralyze you into silence. As author Os Guinness writes, "We should always give an honest answer to honest questions, but we should know from the start that we can never give complete and convincing answers to every question."[2] Remember, faith is a gift from God. Your role is simply to (1) retell the story of the gospel clearly, accurately, and convincingly; (2) try to eliminate any roadblocks or stumbling blocks from their minds that may keep them from understanding what Christ did for them; and (3) bring questions to their minds that show their need for a Savior.

Here are four points that should help you feel more prepared to deal with *any* objection that could come your way.

1. Remember that your presence, this conversation, and your winsome attitude form a strong apologetic for the gospel.

It happens much less often than you'd imagine, but sometimes a gospel conversation does turn hostile and testy. That's why, throughout this book, we've emphasized the importance of treating other people with respect. When you do this, it diffuses much of the tension should someone ever grow frustrated with you or belligerent in refuting the claims you're making.

Think about it: when two friends talk, they may ask questions of each other and challenge each other's ideas, but their tone of voice rarely escalates into anger or offense. As a witness to the gospel, you should expect people to raise questions the way it normally happens in relationships, but a friendly demeanor can keep things loving, caring, and positive. Consider how Jesus faced his critics and how belittling and threatening they could

---

[2] Guinness, *Fool's Talk*, 17 (see chap. 6, n. 1).

sometimes be. But in the end, one of the crucifying soldiers concluded, "Truly this man was the Son of God!" (Matt 27:54).

2. The Bible never suggests that a Christian must be able to answer all questions a skeptic or inquirer may ask.

The Bible is not a reference book for all the questions a person might ask about life. Some people treat it as if it were, or as if it should be, but it's not. There are many things about God and about life in general that we'd all like to know, but which the Bible doesn't come right out and answer. Even the things it *does* address are not always handed to us with fill-in-the-blank simplicity. The Bible can be a complicated book, touching on subjects that even the most learned theologians have difficulty understanding and explaining.

But let the Bible do what it does for all of us. Its purpose is to teach us about God's plan for redeeming this broken world. Nowhere else can you find a story that makes sense of our deepest longings and frustrations. There's more than enough in the Scriptures you already know to satisfactorily explain the love that God shows to us in Christ, even to those who demand that you explain everything to them.

So, you shouldn't feel compelled to give an answer on every possible subject. Your faithfulness as an evangelist doesn't require you to have an answer to every question a person could pose. This doesn't mean you shouldn't try to share your wisdom and best answers where appropriate, but there are a myriad of topics to which the Bible doesn't conclusively speak, or which you simply may not have studied or know enough to speak about.

Memorize the following four sentences, because we promise you they'll come in handy.

- "That's a good question. I don't know the answer to it."
- "That's an interesting question. Let me do a little research or talk with someone, and I'll get back with you about it."

These responses will help you deal with complex issues. Their power is in their honesty. They allow you to affirm someone's question without getting into a circular debate. Most important, their implication is that you value this relationship, and you don't want to stop this conversation.

3. The gospel, not your answers, is the power of God for salvation.

Paul said, "I am not ashamed of the gospel, because it is the power of God for salvation to everyone who believes" (Rom 1:16). Every witness needs to remember this promise. Paul's confidence was not in his own wisdom or ability, wise and able though he was. The gospel itself, he knew, would forever be God's power for salvation, not Paul's skill at defending it. As he said to the Corinthians, "I decided to know nothing among you except Jesus Christ and him crucified" (1 Cor 2:2). He knew the clear gospel would always be enough.

It's possible that you could answer every question a skeptic might ask and they would still refuse to follow Jesus. Yet it's also possible for a person to become a Christian without you adequately dealing with any of their questions. Your task as a witness is simply to share the gospel and trust God to unleash his power to save through it.

4. Unanswered questions rarely keep someone from trusting Christ.

Consider the following statements: (1) You are a Christian, and there are things about the Christian faith you don't completely understand. (2) You are a Christian, and the things you don't understand did not keep you from trusting Christ.

All true? Yes.

So when someone asks you a question that you don't think you can adequately answer, don't panic. If you're a Christian, you know from firsthand experience that the answer to that question is not necessary for salvation. You want to be help-ful, of course. You want to do everything you can do, as we've said, to remove any obstacles that are keeping someone from understanding the greatness of the gospel. But the question for which a person is perhaps demanding an answer is not the single thing that's keeping them from trusting Christ, we assure you.

Several years ago, one of us was discussing the Bible to a group of young men. Most were Christians; a few were inter-ested seekers. At one point, a new guy came in and joined us. And I could tell—sometimes you can just tell—he was a skeptic.

I opened to the book of Genesis and started to explain the story of creation, highlighting that God is the Creator, but his creation had rebelled against him. As soon as I made that state-ment, the young man interrupted and said, "I'm a scientist. Can you explain to me how this relates to the facts of science?"

I told him I *wasn't* a scientist and so I probably could not answer his questions adequately, but that the Bible was clear: God is the Creator of everything around us.

"Well, I don't believe that," he said.

Bit of a pause. Then I said, "I think you've misunderstood something. I'm not here to make you believe anything. My only goal is to make sure you understand what the Bible teaches about God's purpose for this world and your life. Now, whether you believe it or not is up to you. I wish you would, of course. But I won't try to force you."

In other words, *I'll still be your friend.*

And that's the real difference between evangelism that freaks you out and the kind of evangelism that's grounded in making friends and building relationships. You share your story. You're respectful of other people. You listen and converse. And you hope they'll come to faith in Jesus. But if someone doesn't want the free ice cream, that's okay. *You can still be friends.*

Evangelism takes the long view on relationships. Someone else's "no" doesn't mean "no more friendship." Even if you never see a certain friend, coworker, or family member become a Christian, your relationship with that person still has value as the place where faith in Christ might even yet be found.

Love people because of who they are, not what they can become. Love them because God loves them. Love them because they're people for whom he's done a great work so that they can enjoy relationship with him. And through these authentic relationships—these "we can still be friends" relationships—the gospel will always find its way back into the conversation.

CHAPTER 8

Evangelism Happens on Purpose

We cared so much for you that we were pleased to share with you not only the gospel of God but also our own lives, because you had become dear to us.

—1 Thessalonians 2:8

Principle #8

A Jesus-sharing lifestyle starts with a plan to
share Jesus as a part of everyday living.

At various points in our lives, we all identify goals we want to achieve. Maybe it's saving money for a family vacation, or losing weight, or reading through the Bible in a year. The loftier the goal, the more planning is required. Because if we fail to plan, as they say, we plan to fail.

So in this closing chapter, we want to help you establish a plan for putting into practice all the things we have been discussing in this book—a plan for becoming comfortable sharing Jesus without freaking out.

Most people don't follow through with the goals they set. There are many reasons for these failures. But of all the reasons we give for why we don't exercise, why we don't eat right, or why we don't change our spending habits so we can get out of debt, one reason outranks them all.

We don't do it because it's not really as important to us as we say it is.

My (Steve's) son was diagnosed with leukemia at age ten. And when he began chemotherapy, he didn't miss a dose of drugs. Every day, twice a day for five and a half years, he had to take chemotherapy at home. For most of that time, my wife or I also took him every week for chemo infusions at the hospital. I promise you, he didn't do any of it because it made him feel good or because he enjoyed all the toxic chemicals doctors injected in his sick little body to fight his deadly disease. In fact, he hated every minute of it. But he still did it. Because it meant living. Living was what was most important to him.

For a while we relocated our family from North Carolina to Seattle, leaving two children behind, so our son could participate in a clinical trial. Did we do it because we liked paying out the tremendous expense of cancer treatment? Why would we put up with that level of disruption to our family? Why would we stake so much investment into an uncertain outcome? We did it because our son's survival was that important to us.

Since you've stuck with us here to the end, sharing Jesus with others must be highly important to you. You're willing to plan for it and work your plan. You're willing to step out there and do it. You're not content just reading about it and talking about it, even praying about it. You're ready to *do* something about it.

Because like an athlete lifting weights, or a musician practicing scales, or a student spending entire evenings in the library—when you discover something that's of life-changing importance to you, you'll start developing the habits that put you in position to achieve it.

When it comes to sharing Jesus, we think one of those people is you.

So, we believe we'll get your immediate buy-in to Principle #8: *A Jesus-sharing lifestyle starts with a plan to share Jesus as a part of everyday living.*

First Things First

Before going any further, we should clarify that we are not setting out a simple 1-2-3, follow-these-steps prescription for developing an evangelistic lifestyle. That's for *you* to pray and work through. As you place yourself at the Lord's full disposal and develop a rhythm of life that focuses on your spiritual formation as a witness, you will begin to see ways God can use you. However, with this in mind, we do want to make some general points throughout this chapter that can serve as pillars for putting your own plan together.

To begin with, we want to encourage you to focus on the future. You can't change the past, but you can plan tomorrow.

You're probably not unlike a lot of us, who have committed ourselves to sharing Jesus more faithfully but then found it a real struggle to maintain this commitment, too often failing to seize the opportunities the Lord provided. But if you keep focusing on past failure, you will become immobilized by those times when you didn't share the gospel, letting guilt prevent you from pressing ahead.

Also, you cannot allow the enormity of the task to leave you even more overwhelmed. This concern reminds us of a story we heard about a little boy walking down the beach, throwing starfish back into the water. A man came up to him and said, "Son, this beach is littered with stranded starfish. Do you really think you can make a difference?"

The little boy picked up another starfish and tossed it into the waves, saying, "I think I made a difference for that one."

The world is filled with people who need Jesus, but we cannot reach them all single-handedly. Our responsibility is to share the good news of salvation with those whom God places in our lives. Focus on your context and be present in those relationships, because that's where you can be a faithful witness. Let go of the past and walk ahead toward becoming the man or woman God made you to be—a participant in the gospel of Jesus Christ who faithfully retells his or her story in the everyday places where you find yourself.

Think of what God has given you to fulfill your mission. Take out a sheet of paper, or use the blank pages in the back of this book, and create three columns labeled this way: *Giftedness, Calling, Opportunities.*

- Under the subhead *Giftedness,* list everything you understand to be your gift: spiritual gifts, talents, natural skills. Also include "life gifts," such as your education, experiences, family, areas of strength and insight. All these assets contribute to who you are and what you can be. These are gifts from God.

- Under *Calling,* fill this space with things you're passionate about. What moves you emotionally? What brings you joy? What makes you angry? What would you be willing to die for? What have you done that's given you deep satisfaction? Each of these answers factors into your calling. God has shaped your life in such a way that you can't ignore these passions.

- Under *Opportunities,* list your occupation, your hobbies, as well as some of the events that typically fill your calendar. You may wish you had a different job, could pursue different activities, or were able to enjoy other kinds of everyday experiences. But when you think this way, you're missing the fact that God has established you as his ambassador right where you are, with *your* opportunities.

Now go back and circle one item in each column that brings to mind the name of a person you know who is not a Christian. Pray that God would use this gift, calling, or opportunity to create an evangelistic encounter between you and this person. This is a step toward sharing Jesus as you were born to do it.

As we've been repeating throughout this book, the story of the gospel is God's desire to have relationship with humanity. Jesus was born, died, was raised from the dead, and ascended to the Father so that all who receive him can enjoy an eternal relationship with him. But this story you've embraced is not only about *your* salvation; it's the message of salvation for *everyone*. To enjoy the Christian life means sharing this story of Jesus with everybody.

When you're singing with joy on Sundays about the salvation you've received in Christ, realize what your worship is calling you to do. It means you can't remain tight-lipped when you're at the job site on Monday or with your fellow parents in the bleachers on Tuesday night. The privilege of being God's child comes with the privilege of sharing his message.

In that passage from Luke 24 where Jesus appeared to his disciples after his resurrection—the time when he "opened their minds to understand the Scriptures" (v. 45)—he also said this:

> "This is what is written: The Messiah would suffer and rise from the dead the third day, and repentance for forgiveness of sins would be proclaimed in his name to all the nations, beginning at Jerusalem. You are witnesses of these things." (vv. 46–48)

Jesus didn't say the gospel was only about his death and resurrection; it's about the proclamation of that truth by the people he's redeemed. Until there's a retelling of the story, the story is not complete. So, thank you for being someone who's caught a vision for the centrality of evangelism in your Christian life.

Because until we find our purpose in sharing that story, we've badly misunderstood what the story is all about.

Planting and Watering

The reason none of this exhortation should result in freaking out is because the gospel story is designed for you to retell amid the ordinary rhythm of your life. *Lifestyle evangelism.* This doesn't mean you can just be lazy about sharing Jesus, as though you're sitting around waiting for some kind of inspiration to strike. It is also not an excuse for you to refuse to engage in a verbal witness. The challenge is that you watch for opportunities to talk about Jesus even as you're conversing with someone about comic books or tractor parts or parenting ordeals or couponing tips. In the same way that you tell your coworkers over lunch about your experience with finding a good fishing spot, you tell them about your experience with the gospel. Learning to practice lifestyle evangelism doesn't require you to change either your location or your vocation, only your narration.

And along with this change in narration comes a change in expectation. Think of it the way Paul thought of it: as a process of planting and watering.

Paul considered himself a partner with other believers in sharing the gospel. One of those partners was a man named Apollos. Apollos shows up in the book of Acts—in Ephesus in Acts 18, in Corinth in Acts 19—as well as in a couple of Paul's letters. Both men were obviously dynamic evangelists. But in 1 Corinthians 3, Paul commented on his work with Apollos by using an agricultural metaphor to teach something vital about how evangelism is supposed to operate.

> What then is Apollos? What is Paul? They are servants through whom you believed, and each has the role the

Lord has given. I planted, Apollos watered, but God gave the growth. (vv. 5–6)

In the specific context of Corinth, Paul had planted the seed of the gospel before traveling on to other cities to evangelize elsewhere. Then Apollos came behind him and watered the spiritual seed Paul had planted. Neither Paul nor Apollos was there to reap the full harvest as it came in (as non-Christians believed and trusted Christ). But the two of them understood their role as sowers and cultivators of the seed. They were each content being part of the germination process that was ultimately God's responsibility to bring to fruition.

What does this "planting and watering" look like in your own life? It looks like living out the gospel in your friendships, taking opportunities to talk about Jesus as those moments naturally arise. You're planting a seed. That's all. And once it's in the ground of that person's mind and heart, you have no way of knowing what's happening there.

Planting and watering also means that some of the people with whom you share Jesus have already heard the gospel from another person or persons. You cannot know all that the Lord is doing or has already done. That's not your job either. God has called you only to pour water on the seed, to participate with him in bringing that plant up out of the ground. If the harvest is still a ways off, that's okay. You've done your part today simply by helping things along.

So as you consider your plan, become intentional with the relationships you identified in the Concentric Circles exercise from the previous chapter. Write down those people's names somewhere that will be readily accessible to you. Set a reminder on your phone to pray for them every day. Ask God to give you an opportunity to say something to them about the gospel, no matter how small. "Help me plant a seed, Lord, or water a seed that's already planted."

That's evangelism. That's the ongoing process of giving something new for a non-Christian to consider, all while being fully aware that their repentance and faith will likely take some time. It probably won't occur until after a long pattern of living and speaking the gospel into that relationship. Lots of planting. Lots of watering.

But unless you're content with this dynamic, rather than being disappointed and discouraged in your evangelism efforts if they don't result in a harvesting event, you'll have a hard time staying confident sharing Jesus.

Do the Right Thing

My family and I have been part of the childhood-cancer community for nearly ten years. Within that community, as you can expect, people are dealing with significant pain—emotional, physical, spiritual. Parents of children and teens with cancer face a lifetime of fear and struggle even when their kids survive. From the moment a parent hears "Your child has cancer," even good news is tainted with pain. From watching their child suffer, to worrying that the next test will bring terrible news, everything changes for families in this community.

What's the job of a Christian, then, who finds himself ministering to families like these? He obviously knows they need physical help. Many of them need financial assistance. They also need emotional support. They need a lot of things. And, yes, they need Jesus.

But isn't it disingenuous to reach out to them with assistance as sort of a bait and switch? "I'll pretend to care about you and your child, but the only real reason I'm really interested in you is to tell you about Jesus"? People can see right through the hollowness and pretension of those kinds of do-gooders. Gospel presentations don't work there. *Relationships do.*

The right thing for a Christian in such situations is to love people where they're hurting. Don't stalk them for Jesus;

just build a real relationship. Look for ways to be a genuine blessing. Meet their needs. Care for them. Pick up their other kids from school. Buy them gift cards. Send them notes of encouragement. Sit quietly while they cry themselves to sleep. *Be Christian.* Love the Lord with all your heart, and love your neighbor as yourself.

We're not saying that good works, even when done from a Christian motivation, are the same thing as evangelism. No one will learn that God offers salvation through faith in Jesus Christ by our simple acts of kindness and generosity alone. But good works do have an important role to play in Christian evangelism. They serve as a witness to the authenticity of our faith. Helping to meet people's non-spiritual needs is an essential illustration of the story you're hoping to tell.

Then, when a person is ready to listen, you can share Jesus *genuinely* from within the *genuine* relationship you've been developing. Yet even then, don't talk with them about five steps to a happy life with God; simply tell them the story of God at work in Christ . . .

- a God who loves them enough to meet them in their pain.
- a God who hates childhood cancer as much as they do.
- a God who weeps for their child right there alongside them.
- a God who turns weeping into laughter, mourning into joy.

They'll still have questions, for sure. And the basic gospel message won't answer everything, particularly the question of why their child has cancer. But when those individuals want to know what God offers them in the midst of their suffering, you'll have a story you can tell them . . . all because you've prayerfully done the right things for them, simply because it was the right thing to do.

Prayer and Evangelism

Being a faithful witness is a prayer adventure as well. Prayer deepens your relationship with God and enables you to serve and share from the overflow of your heart. Prayer allows you to bring to him the many needs of others, both physical and spiritual. Talk to God about people before you talk to people about God.

We encourage you to pray for at least four things every day.[1]

1. Pray for boldness.

Acts 4 presents a story about the persecution of Jesus's early followers. Government officials forbade them from witnessing for Christ, threatening them with imprisonment and physical harm if they refused to obey. Then what happened?

> When they heard this, they raised their voices together to God. . . . "Lord, consider their threats, and grant that your servants may speak your word with all boldness." (vv. 24, 29)

Boldness. Our friend Preston Nix, a professor of evangelism at New Orleans Baptist Theological Seminary, says boldness in evangelism is simply going one step beyond your comfort zone.

As you pray, ask for boldness to talk with others about Christ.

2. Pray for power.

Paul, in describing the "full armor of God" (Eph 6:11), included prayer as one of its key elements (v. 18). Then, in conclusion, he asked the Ephesian Christians to pray for his witness, for the bold proclamation of the gospel (vv. 19–20).

---

[1] The following section is adapted from Alvin Reid, *Evangelism Handbook: Biblical, Spiritual, Intentional, Missional* (Nashville: B&H, 2009), chapters 10–11.

As seen in Acts 1:8, the Holy Spirit empowers our witness. He works in the evangelistic conversation from both directions: he supplies the witnesses themselves with opportunity, reminding them of the right words to speak; and he convicts sinners of their sin, helping them understand the claims of the gospel. Pray for God's power to always be at work in you.

3. Pray for partners.

"The harvest is abundant," Jesus said to his disciples, "but the workers are few. Therefore," he added, "pray to the Lord of the harvest to send out workers into his harvest" (Luke 10:2). As you're praying for the Holy Spirit to empower your own witness, pray also that God would awaken other believers to the spiritual needs of those around them. As Jesus pointed out, there are people ready to hear the gospel; their need is for someone to tell them about it.

Part of your praying, of course, should be asking God to call people into international missions, where the fields remain full. But pray as well for God to call the Christians who live across the street to become his witnesses. Think of how different your neighborhood, your workplace, your school, and the community around you would be if more believers were sharing Jesus regularly. Ask God for helpers.

4. Pray for people.

Pray regularly for those who need Jesus. Ask God to

- open their eyes to spiritual things (2 Cor 4:4);
- give them ears to hear (Matt 13:15), faith to believe (Acts 20:21), and the will to respond to the gospel (Rom 10:9);
- send a faithful witness into their lives (Luke 10:2); and
- help you build genuine relationships with unbelievers (1 Cor 9:22–23).

Don't be surprised—you may be the answer to your own prayer about God's sending a faithful witness!

Yes!

Even if the thought of sharing Jesus with someone still sounds a bit daunting to you, here's the truth of it: the more you enjoy your relationship with him, the more you'll recognize opportunities for helping others enjoy him as well. So while you may not be entirely past the freaking out stage as you sit here today, we think we know you well enough by now to say it's time to start asking yourself, "What do I do if I share Jesus with someone, and they say 'yes'?"

Yes!—go ahead and be prepared for that. Be ready for one of your gospel conversations to result in a friend or coworker saying to you, "All right, so what do I need to do if I want to become a Christian?"—because you sure don't want to be caught with a deer-in-the-headlights look in your eyes, saying, "Hmm. Good question."

There's no magic formula for guiding someone to become a Christian. The best way to get ready for it is by looking to see how believers in the Bible responded to this question or to similar questions. Thankfully, Scripture provides us with several instances to learn from.

One particularly helpful encounter occurs in Acts 16, when Paul and his traveling companion Silas were confined to jail in the city of Philippi. You'll remember how the Lord caused an earthquake to strike around midnight while Paul and Silas were "praying and singing hymns to God, and the prisoners were listening to them" (v. 25). In the darkness and confusion, after Paul assured the jailer they weren't making a break for it, the astonished man rushed up to them and asked, "Sirs, what must I do to be saved?" (v. 30).

Notice what they said to him. It's so simple.

"Believe in the Lord Jesus, and you will be saved." (v. 31)

Keep in mind, when someone wishes to become a Christian, the work is already done. Their desire to respond to the genuine story of the gospel is itself the mark of conversion. Paul and Silas certainly understood this, and essentially said to the man, "There's nothing you must do other than believe."

When a gospel conversation ends with someone asking how they can be saved, start with an answer as simple as "Believe in Jesus as Lord." There's really no more complicated formula or multistep process required.

But that's not all we see happening in this Acts 16 account, and we can pick up a second layer of practical advice as we read it. Notice that Paul and Silas went home with the jailer afterward (vv. 32, 34). They shared with him and his entire family what being a Christian meant. In other words, they chose to *deepen the relationship.* They didn't merely lead the jailer in a sinner's prayer and rush off to their next evangelistic encounter. They sought to help him take steps toward growing in Christ.

Even people who receive Christ in response to a onetime gospel presentation are sure to experience their new relationship with God to the fullest as they begin actively participating in authentic relationships with other Christians. The story of the gospel is about a relationship—a new relationship with God—a story that encompasses *all* our relationships, making all of them new.

So whenever you tell God's story, you're inviting someone into a new manner of relating, both to him and other people. And when that person responds to the gospel story in faith, desiring to become a Christian, you now have opportunity to walk with them into this new relationship by promising you'll stay in relationship with them yourself.

You want the conversations to keep going forward.

So, how about doing this when someone asks you how to become a Christian (and they will!):

- *First, pray FOR the person.* Stop right in the middle of your conversation and pray for them. Pray that they'll understand the gospel accurately. And thank God for bringing them to this place of recognizing the wonderful work of God in Christ on their behalf.
- *Second, pray WITH them.* There's nothing wrong with helping someone find the words to articulate their newfound faith. In fact, there's everything right with it! Again, becoming a Christian doesn't involve a mantra or magic prayer, just an expression of trust and faith in Jesus Christ. Feel free to use a sinner's prayer you're familiar with, or create one on the spot.
- *Third, pray ALONGSIDE them.* Like Paul and Silas, every Christian who has the privilege of being in relationship with a new believer should invest heavily in that relationship. The church—the community of Christians— is a family. And you, as their brother or sister, can love enjoying Jesus right along with them in worship, study, prayer, and ministry.

The gospel relationship isn't over when someone becomes a Christian. Conversion is just the beginning of the Christian life that you and that new believer now share with one another.

Satisfied Customer, Not a Salesperson

You were born (again) to do evangelism. You share the gospel as a satisfied customer, not a commissioned salesperson.

A good salesman can sell you a car. When you walk onto his lot, he knows how to put you into a vehicle. You sit in the front seat while he gives you the rundown on the car's attractive features—its snazzy control center, its entertainment system, its network of cameras and sensors, its heated seats. He pops the hood to show you its sleek, powerful, factory-polished engine, and he points out the car's many other desirable advantages and benefits. He makes it sound irresistible. And he truly believes in what he's selling. But while he may indeed be genuinely interested in getting you the best car for the best price, he really has only one overarching desire: he wants the sale. And whether *you* buy it or the next guy buys it, doesn't really matter—as long as someone takes that vehicle off his lot today.

Let's say, though, you decide to buy. You drive your new car (or new-to-you car) to work the next day, and you're thrilled with it. You're so happy with your purchase. One of your coworkers walks over to you as you're getting out, and asks what you have there. *New car.* You open the door and show him the same features and accessories as the salesman did. You hope he likes it. But you're not trying to *sell* him on all these bells and whistles. You may not even remember what kind of engine the salesman said it had. "As long as it gets me to work and back," you say, "I'm good."

Evangelism is more like the office parking lot part of this story than the new car dealership part of this story. You talk eagerly about what you've been blessed enough to bring home with you and call your own. You share what your experience with it has been like. You tell a few of the things you understand about it but admit you're still learning some of what it does. If the other person happens to be in the market for a new car, you know a good place where he can get one. But there's no pressure to turn him into a buyer, and if he's not interested in getting one for himself, that's fine. Even if he doesn't like *your* new car, it's fine. *You* like it, and you're really satisfied with it. And in the future, if your friend *does* decide he'd like to know where you got such a good car, you'd certainly love talking with him about it and giving a recommendation.

Wouldn't it be great if your friend could have this experience too?

God has given you the incredible opportunity to participate in his mission of reconciliation through announcing the good news of Jesus Christ to the world, starting with those who are right around you. Jesus said to his disciples, "As the Father has sent me, I also send you" (John 20:21). By sharing Jesus without freaking out—simply sharing the gospel story—you're able to live that sent life.

APPENDIX I
An Evangelism Catechism

A catechism is a tool for teaching using questions and answers. Throughout the book, we have asked several questions that fit together as a catechism about evangelism, capturing the essence of the book's message. The four questions establish the foundation for effectively sharing Jesus without freaking out. As you ask and answer these four simple questions, they will help shape a life of faithful communication of the good news of Jesus Christ.

Q 1. What is the purpose of evangelism?

A 1. The purpose of evangelism is to retell the story of the gospel of Jesus Christ according to the written text of Scripture in a way that our listeners can understand it.

Let's unpack that answer.

Sharing Jesus does not mean we simply give an account of our own religious experiences. We can misunderstand the experiences we have. One person may believe—truly believe—they have been escorted into heaven and want to share that experience with other people. Someone else may have had a dream with a religious revelation. Sharing those personal stories is not evangelism. Instead, evangelism is retelling *the* story of the Bible, in which God creates a place, creates people, and creates a means for people to enjoy him forever. Evangelism is recounting to people the story of the Bible.

Evangelism requires explanation of the gospel, not simply statements about the gospel. It is true that Jesus died for sinners, but if our listener has little to no idea of who Jesus is, or what sin means, or how atonement works according to the Bible, we are reading from a menu in a foreign language. We want to share Jesus in a way that is understandable.

Q 2. What is the relationship between evangelism and conversion?
A 2. Conversion comes only through hearing the gospel of Jesus Christ with understanding.

Conversion, also called salvation, is a spiritual work by God alone. There are a number of constituent components to conversion, such as repentance, faith, regeneration, re-creation, adoption, etc. The only way people can be saved is by the hearing of the gospel with understanding. In other words, evangelism is the process by which God brings about conversion. Romans 10 describes the process like this: a Christian explains the gospel to a non-Christian. The non-Christian affirms the truthfulness of that story. Then the non-Christian believes in Jesus Christ and is converted.

Evangelism is not about [you] saving people. Evangelism is helping people understand the means by which they might be saved.

Q 3. What is the relationship between good works and evangelism?
A 3. When we genuinely love people and meet their needs, we build authentic relationships through which we share the gospel.

It is tempting to substitute helping people for sharing Jesus with them. Everyone is willing to have some help with their problems. For as long as missionaries have existed, they have struggled with the role of good works in their evangelism. It is no less true for ordinary Christians looking to share Jesus in their own contexts.

One question we need to consider as we think about the relationship between good works and evangelism is, "Has the Christian offered a faithful witness to the gospel of Jesus Christ because he or she has helped meet the needs of a non-Christian?" Take a homeless shelter, for example. Is providing food and shelter to a homeless family the same thing as evangelizing them? We have defined sharing Jesus as retelling the story of the gospel so that people can become Christians by receiving that message. Defining evangelism in this way means that showing the love of God, even with a Christian motivation, is not itself evangelism. Evangelism is communicating a story. No one will learn that God offers salvation through faith in Jesus Christ by simple acts of kindness and generosity. So good works, in and of themselves, are not evangelism.

But words without works are hollow.

Q 4. What is the Christian's role in evangelism?

A 4. As Christians, we retell the gospel of Jesus through a life that reflects God's work and a message that accurately explains what that work is.

We must share the good news of God's work in Christ to other people as clearly as possible with both our lives and our lips. It is not possible to have an answer for every question someone might ask or resolve every objection unbelievers would have to becoming a Christian. The point in evangelism is not to win an argument. Our objective is not to be proven right and the unbeliever proven wrong, as though the reason someone is not a Christian is because that person has the wrong information.

Our goal is to help people learn the story of Jesus and have an opportunity to believe that story or not. Don't let people reject a truncated or inaccurate story about Jesus; at least let them see and hear the whole story before they choose to reject it.

APPENDIX II
Sharing the Story of the Gospel

God's story and its impact on your life can give you confidence to share Jesus in any situation.

One of our goals in writing this book has been to eliminate some of the stress that many Christians feel when they think about evangelism. When you became a Christian, you received everything you needed to make you an effective evangelist. Not only were your sins forgiven, but you also became a new creation (2 Cor 5:17) and were filled with the Holy Spirit. It's not necessary for you to become someone else—Billy Graham, John Piper, or even one of us—in order to share Jesus. In some ways, this book has been your journey down the proverbial Yellow Brick Road into Oz. Like the Scarecrow, the Tin Man, and the Cowardly Lion, you've learned that the thing you wanted most, you've had all along.

When I (Scott) attended seminary in New Orleans, I took a course on personal evangelism. One of the major components of the class required students to memorize a thirty- to forty-five-minute gospel presentation. For our final exam, each student sat with a proctor and recited the entire presentation, along with Scripture verses. We were docked points for each mistake.

In preparation for this exam, students volunteered to assist local churches in their weekly visitations. In theory, these contacts allowed us to practice the presentations several times a month. The one exception to this rule was for students who volunteered to assist the Vieux Carre Baptist Church. This church was in the French Quarter, and students who volunteered there would spend time each week on the streets in downtown New Orleans. Our professor told us that students who helped this church would have more opportunities to share the gospel than any other students, but none of these experiences would help with the final exam. "You'll still be responsible for knowing the entire presentation," we were told.

When class was over, my roommate and I sprinted to the front of the classroom to volunteer for that church. The professor was correct. We spent months in the French Quarter, on and around Bourbon Street. We shared Jesus with hundreds of people and used dozens of evangelism tools, but to the best of my knowledge, none of us ever used the forty-five-minute presentation. To this day, I still remember most of that presentation. (I've even used it to share Jesus.) But one of my main takeaways from that semester was that no single method is effective in all situations. However, we also learned that it's helpful to have some practical suggestions or advice to support the theories.

As we conclude this book, we want to provide a few helpful guidelines for sharing Jesus without freaking out. This is not a how-to chapter. Our purpose here is to suggest some handles to go along with the principles we've provided—even though we know there's no surefire method that guarantees success.

In this chapter, we'll give you some simple counsel for sharing the gospel story in various situations. We'll also give simple guidelines for sharing your own story (your personal testimony) to help others understand the impact your faith in Jesus has made in your life.

We hope you've noticed that one of our primary goals has been to show that the Bible is a powerful tool for evangelism. While we appreciate (and have used) many of the other tools people use for sharing Jesus, we want you to be comfortable with the story of the Bible so that you can be ready to share casually and conversationally in any situation. In this section, we want to show you how to share Jesus using the story line of the Bible—creation to redemption—as well as smaller stories in the Bible.

Sharing from the Story Line of Scripture

Evangelism, using the overarching story of Scripture, is not new; in fact, it's as old as the New Testament itself. Sharing Christ in a casual, relational way, taking advantage of the narrative of Scripture, is something we see Christians in the New Testament doing.

Take a few minutes and look at the following passages:

- Acts 2:14–41
- Acts 3:11–26 .
- Acts 7:2–53
- Acts 17:22–31

Each of these passages contains an example of early Christians sharing Jesus. In each encounter, the evangelist is addressing different groups of people in different settings. The encounters begin differently, but they tell the same basic story—the story we've summarized throughout the book.

- There is a God who created this world.
- God is good and has good plans for his creation.
- Humans disobeyed God and have fallen away from his original plan.
- God, because of his great love, has made a way for this broken relationship to be mended; he sent his Son Jesus.
- The proper response is to believe and be made right with God.

Notice that each of these evangelistic encounters ends the same way: with an opportunity for the hearer to accept Jesus. Every time, someone says yes to the appeal and others reject it. But in each, the evangelist has accomplished his role. He's provided information and opportunity for the hearers to move one step closer to Jesus.

Sharing Jesus without freaking out is just this simple, just this flexible. You know the story. So, like these early Christians, you can tell it in most any situation.

We don't measure success based on the completion of a preset outline. Effective evangelism happens when we meet the other person at the point of their question and show how it fits into the gospel story. We offer them a chance to respond to the good news.

You may say, "I see how this happened in the Bible, but how might this work in my life?"

Imagine, for example, you're talking with a friend about the political situation in our country. Your friend is concerned because he or she believes that things seem out of control. They're afraid all these changes will make a world unlivable for our children. Keep in mind that it doesn't matter if your friend's political views are to the left or right of yours. Your hope is not to convert your friend to become a Republican or Democrat. You only want to share with them the hope found in Jesus. The good news is that your friend's concerns fit perfectly into the gospel.

If you want to see how this might work, look at Psalm 2 for an example:

- God created a world that was very good.
- But Psalm 2 describes a world in which "the nations rage and the peoples plot in vain" (v. 1). It also says, "The kings of the earth take their stand, and the rulers conspire together against the LORD and his Anointed One" (v. 2). Human selfishness and sinfulness have caused great pain and suffering. This includes the selfishness of politicians and citizens as well as the suffering this causes for everyone.

APPENDIX II: SHARING THE STORY OF THE GOSPEL

- But verses 7 and 8 remind us that God sent his Son to bring peace into the world and to give peace to those who live in a broken world.
- Finally, God has promised in verse 12 that anyone who places their faith in his Son can have peace and confidence, even in a society that seems to be falling apart.

Can you see how each of these points follow the plotline of Scripture?

Can you imagine how this conversation might flow?

More importantly, can you see yourself having this conversation with a friend or family member?

Let's look at another example:

Imagine you're talking with a friend who is suffering because of sin. Maybe they're suffering because of their own bad choices—they've done something incredibly foolish and are suffering under the consequences. Perhaps you're talking to a parent who's afraid because their child is making bad choices. The parent feels hopeless.

Again, this situation fits perfectly within the gospel story. If you want to see how, look at Luke 15, the story of the prodigal son.

- *The pain and brokenness in the world is because people have rebelled against God.* In the story, the rebellious son faces a harsh life as he lives with the penalty and shame of his sin (vv. 13–16).
- *Despite our rebellion, God has not turned his back on us.* The Father is waiting for his son to return (vv. 17–20).
- *God has made a way for us (and our wayward children) to be forgiven and be in a right relationship with him.*
- *God allows us to bring our brokenness and sinfulness to him. Anyone can respond to his invitation to trust Jesus and be forgiven.* In this story, Jesus shows that our heavenly Father receives repentant sinners with joy and welcomes them into his family (vv. 21–24).

Again, can you see how each of these points follow the biblical story line?

Can you see how each meets your friend at the point of pain and serves as a source of pleasure?

Take a few minutes and think about some of the people you listed during our Concentric Circles exercise in chapter 7. What do you know about their lives that might serve as an opportunity to share with them using the story of Scripture?

Remember, there are many entrance points into this conversation. The more familiar you become with the biblical story and biblical examples, the more prepared you will feel. However, you are already prepared to share Jesus without freaking out.

Sharing Jesus through the Stories and Sayings of the Bible

It is also possible to share Jesus with others by using Bible stories to launch you into a gospel conversation. I (Scott) remember talking with a family from Iran. The man told me he didn't think his family could become Christians because people from their country were not allowed to convert. I told him I thought that was sad. Then I said, "You know, people from Iran were some of the first people in the world to recognize who Jesus was and to worship him."

For the next ten or fifteen minutes, the family listened as I talked to them about the birth of Jesus and the visits of the Magi (wise men from Persia, or Iran). When I finished, they asked if there were any other stories in the Bible about their country. I told them about Daniel in the lion's den and about Shadrach, Meshach, and Abednego. All of these stories took place in Persia, which is in the same area of the world as modern Iran.

My goal in telling these stories was to show that the Bible spoke directly to the question they were asking: *Is it possible for someone like me to be right with God?*

On another occasion, I was talking to a group of refugees about the difficult nature of their lives. They were telling me about the frustration of being insecure about the future, of feeling like they were pawns in someone else's game. One of the men said, "You know, I just found out that if we can get married to someone from this country and stay married for five years, we could become permanent citizens."

Now I wasn't sure if that was true or not, but I knew acting on it wouldn't be his best decision. I said, "I don't know about that. I heard a saying one time that it was better to live on the corner of a roof than in a house with a quarrelsome wife" (see Prov 21:9). They thought that was about the funniest thing they'd ever heard. One of the guys said, "Where did you hear that?"

I told him it was from the Bible. Then he said, "Are there any more sayings like that in the Bible?"

I said, "Of course there are." So I started from there and talked with them about Jesus and his plan for their lives. By using that proverb, I was able to show how the gospel spoke directly to one of their points of brokenness.

Over the years, as we've talked to people about using Bible stories and sayings as points of entry into the gospel story, they often respond by saying, "I'm not as familiar with the Bible as you are. I could never do that."

Well, first, we don't believe that's true. If you've been in church for any length of time, you're already familiar with dozens of Bible stories and pithy sayings. Let's do a quick exercise. Take out a piece of paper, or use one of the blank pages in this book, and make a list of as many Bible stories and sayings as you can think of. Don't worry about getting all the details right. Just jot down titles or whole sayings.

How many did you list? Probably more than you thought you knew.

Now, next to each entry, write out different life situations or questions, sources of blessing and brokenness, hopes and fears that these stories might speak to. Don't stress too much over perfection. At this point, you're just building a list of potential resources.

See how easy that was? You are already more prepared than you thought.

Second, in response to the claim that you don't know enough about the Bible to be able to use it when you share Jesus, we would simply (but lovingly) say, "Well, that's an easy problem to fix. If you really want to."

The Bible is a book. If you are reading this book, you can read the Bible. If you struggle to read the Bible, there are apps for your phone that make it possible to listen to the Bible as an audiobook. In other words, we're convinced that anyone can learn the Bible and learn to use it as a tool for sharing Jesus.

Sharing Your Story

Throughout this book we've highlighted the fact that the gospel is a story. We've also pointed out that it's not merely a historical story, something in the past. The gospel is also present tense; it is a story you're living in right now.

One of the most helpful evangelism tools is your personal testimony: *you* telling the story of how the gospel shapes your life. The more comfortable you become with this tool, the more you will discover how useful it can be. You could use your testimony to introduce or conclude your gospel conversations.

There are times when your testimony serves as a real-life illustration. Other times, your testimony can serve as the main content of the conversation. If you wrap up your story with a question like, "Has anything like this ever happened to you?" it can serve as a powerful invitation for others to place their faith in Christ.

Before we go further, we want to provide a few words of warning:

1. Our testimonies do not prove the truthfulness of the gospel. The gospel is true because it is God's story.
2. We need to be careful that we guide others to place their faith in Jesus, not in us. The gospel, not our testimonies, is the power unto salvation.
3. When possible, use Scripture throughout your story. Remember, faith comes by hearing the Word of God.
4. When possible, eliminate technical language. Let your story be a testimony of real life using everyday language.

There are two kinds of testimonies we want to encourage you to use. We've found both of them to be extremely effective in evangelistic conversations. With a little preparation, you can become comfortable with each, and both can be beneficial as you witness.

1. Your salvation story

This is what most people think of when they think about using their personal testimony in evangelism. It's the story of how you learned about your need for Jesus and how you trusted him as your Savior.

This story usually has four key parts:

1. *A brief description of your life before you became a Christian.* This is not a time to relive your past sins. At the same time, don't be intimidated if your testimony doesn't include a dramatic life change because you came to faith at a young age. In this part of your testimony, you are answering the simple question, "Have you been a Christian your whole life?"

Be brief. But take time to show the problems you faced as an unbeliever. Talk about the penalty of sin in your life. You might even choose to begin this part of your story with the sentence, "You know, I haven't always been a Christian."

2. *How you realized that you needed to become a Christian.* What happened to cause you to question your lifestyle and begin to look to Christ? Was there an internal change? Did something

happen in your life? How did God reveal to you that you needed him?

The Bible tells us that every person who isn't a Christian is spiritually dead. God did something in your life that made you aware something wasn't right. This is a very important moment in your testimony. It is the experience the other person may be dealing with currently. Your story can help them understand what's happening and give them a degree of hope.

3. *What steps you took to become a Christian.* Once you realized you needed to be saved, what did you do? Did you pray? Did you read the Bible? Did you go to church?

This is perhaps the most important section of your story. In this section you should provide a clear presentation of the gospel and also give the listener biblical counsel about how to become a Christian. Far too often, a well-meaning evangelist gives bad advice here, using phrases such as "I walked down the aisle of the church," or "I asked Jesus into my heart."

Once you're inside the faith, of course, both of these sentences (and others like them) make sense. But to a non-Christian, these descriptions are not helpful. The better explanation is to use biblical language. "When I realized I was a sinner, I prayed and asked Jesus to save me." Give the details of that prayer. You might be able to supply some of the counsel someone gave you.

In this section of a testimony, we've found it helpful to include some Scripture passages that explain what it means to become a Christian. Consider saying something like, "I realized God loved me so much that he did everything necessary for my salvation. If I would believe in him, I could have eternal life."

You might also say, "For my whole life I thought I had to be good in order for God to love me. But I finally realized it wasn't by my works that I could be saved. Instead, the Bible says anyone who calls on the name of the Lord can be saved. When I realized that, I bowed my head and I called out in prayer. I asked God to save me from my sins." In this section, you want to present a very clear path to salvation.

4. *How your faith has positively affected your life.* Now that you're a Christian, what has God done for you? Has he given you peace, security, community? Very often the answer to this question can be found in the brokenness of the first three points of this outline.

We can't promise that God will do for others the exact thing he did for us. But on the assurance of God's Word, we can talk about the blessings of salvation.

The challenge here is to help the other person know the benefits of faith and then invite them to trust Christ by asking, "So, has anything like this ever happened to you?"

2. Your situational story

This is the story (or stories) of how your relationship with Jesus has helped you through a situation in your life.

Are you a parent? Has your child walked away from the faith? Has your child been diagnosed with a terminal illness?

Are you a student? Have you felt like a failure? Have you been promoted to your dream job? Have you been afraid of failure . . . or success?

Have you fallen into sin? Are you suffering because of your own stupid or sinful decisions? Are you suffering because of the sin of others? Each of these questions, and thousands more, provide situations that allow you to tell your story of how Jesus makes a difference in the real world in which we live. The power of this type of storytelling is that it enables you to identify with the person you're talking with, and to be a personal witness about how Jesus can help that person right now.

It is not necessary for your situation to perfectly match the situation of the person you're talking with. It is enough for you to be experiencing similar things. I (Steve) have mentioned that my son was diagnosed with leukemia. This life-altering situation has given my family many opportunities to talk with others about the difference our relationship with Jesus has made in our lives.

Obviously, we've been able to talk with families that are experiencing similar trauma. However, we've also discovered that this situation has provided us a chance to talk with couples who are struggling in their marriages. You see, when a child is diagnosed with a terminal illness, the vast majority of marriages end in divorce. There are many reasons for this tragedy: stress, neglect, guilt, even adultery when one spouse looks for support outside the bonds of marriage. Because our marriage has survived this difficult season, my wife and I have been able to talk with dozens of couples who, even though their children have not been diagnosed with a life-threatening disease, are experiencing marriage problems.

These different types of situations have allowed us opportunity to share Jesus with families who are suffering, parents who have lost children, as well as couples who are facing the collapse of their marriage relationships. Our story has allowed us to show the power of the gospel in many different situations.

Your situational story usually consists of three basic points.

1. *Describe the situation.* (Identify with the person to whom you're talking.) In the course of a relationship, a friend will talk with you about a situation or will ask advice on how you handle certain situations in your life. Resist the temptation to play counselor. As noted earlier, when someone shares with you about a crisis that seems too big for them to handle alone, it may be a signal that God is at work in their lives. It may be your invitation to join the Holy Spirit in his work of revealing their need for Jesus.

Talk a bit about a time when you encountered a similar situation in your life. Warning: There is no need to go into great detail; the other person is already living it. It's also not necessary to try convincing the other person that you know how they feel or that your situation was as bad as what they are experiencing. Your goal in this section is to help the other person understand that Jesus is alive and that the gospel can make a difference in real-life crises.

2. *How did Jesus help you survive (thrive) in that specific situation?* Be specific here. How did your relationship with Jesus help you in the situation you just described? This is your testimony of the present, living power of the gospel. Did you gain strength, patience, wisdom, companionship? Did God's forgiveness give you hope? Did God's presence help you endure failure? As you are sharing, keep these three points in mind:

- Don't promise that God will do the exact same thing in the exact same way.
- Point them to the Bible, not your experience, as the source of hope.
- Avoid technical language. When possible, speak plainly about the gospel.

In this section, your goal is to answer the question, "Does the Christian message apply only to life after death? Is there any real hope in this broken world?"

3. *How does the work of the gospel give you hope in other, similar situations?* When David faced Goliath, he was confident that God would help him because he'd experienced God's protection in other situations in life. "The LORD who rescued me from the paw of the lion and the paw of the bear will rescue me from the hand of this Philistine" (1 Sam 17:37).

The living gospel gives us hope as we face different situations. The power of the gospel is that, because of our relationship with Christ, we walk by faith. Our relationship with Jesus affects every area of our lives. Most people who are not Christians don't understand how powerful and dynamic the gospel is. Your story puts skin on the message.

As you read the Bible, you will find many examples of men and women sharing with others about the difference Jesus made in their lives. You, too, can use this powerful evangelism tool.

Take a few minutes and jot down your salvation testimony and several situational testimonies. Remove unnecessary religious language. Practice telling it to a friend or family member who already knows the Lord until you're comfortable talking about your story.

In this appendix, we've provided four practical evangelism tools that can help you share Jesus casually, without freaking out. The more you practice and prepare, the more comfortable you will become using them.

The Eight-Week Challenge

The Eight-Week Challenge is a way for individuals, small groups, and college/seminary students to interact with the teaching and principles found in *Sharing Jesus without Freaking Out*. The purpose of it is to answer the question, so now what? Now that I know to connect the gospel to people's blessing and brokenness, what are the next steps? How do I walk out a life of evangelism in my context?

In this challenge, we're going to make this teaching personal so that at the end of eight weeks, you'll be well on your way to a lifestyle of retelling the story of the good news of God's work reconciling the world to himself in Jesus Christ.

These short, weekly segments were created for normal people with busy lives. In a few minutes each day—whether first thing in the morning, over lunch, or after the kids are in bed—you can walk through the practical steps that will help you establish a lifestyle and mentality for sharing Christ and doing it on a regular basis.

Just like with diet and exercise, a life of evangelism involves a slow change of habits along with intentionality. Be prayerful and diligent but also patient with yourself as you move through the next eight weeks. In order to build new habits into your life, you will be replacing old habits, some of which you've practiced for many years. We will trust the Lord together. As Paul wrote in Phil 1:6, "I am sure of this, that he who started a good work in you will carry it on to completion until the day of Christ Jesus."

Each section is broken into four activities. Take some time each week to work through as much as you can. You'll probably want to have a notebook or electronic document available to record your insights and thoughts.

1. *Scripture Meditation.* Take time to think about the different Bible passages. Reflect often on their meaning. If possible, commit them to memory.

2. *Application.* Work through several questions each day. Record your insights. Seek ways to implement the challenges.

3. *Prayer.* Spend several minutes each day praying through the different topics provided.

4. *Who Is Your One?* Part of this Eight-Week Challenge is to identify at least one person in your circles of concern who you think is not a Christian. We will refer to this person as *your one* throughout the challenge. Each week you'll be challenged to engage in at least one activity to help you influence him or her for Christ.

Our hope and confidence are not in our abilities; rather, they're in the faithful work of God in our lives. Let's begin this eight-week challenge by committing our efforts to the Lord.

Heavenly Father, in your great love you have made a way for sinful people to be forgiven and made part of your eternal family. You have placed in me a desire to be a more faithful and effective witness of your gospel of grace.

I confess to you my insecurities and my weaknesses. Yet I trust your power and faithfulness. Make me the witness I need to be so that many can come to know your love and I can experience a renewed life in Christ.

Amen.

Week 1

*Principle #1: You have all you need to begin
sharing Jesus with other people right now.*

Scriptures for Meditation

"God has not given us a spirit of fear, but one of power, love,
and sound judgment." (2 Tim 1:7)

"Go, therefore, and make disciples of all nations, baptizing
them in the name of the Father and of the Son and of the Holy
Spirit, teaching them to observe everything I have commanded
you." (Matt 28:19–20)

Questions for Reflection and Application

1. What tasks in general are daunting to you?
2. What is it about evangelism that freaks you out?
3. What's the worst thing that could realistically happen
    if you spoke to someone about Jesus this week? (Hint:
    "the worst thing" is probably not going to happen!) Now,
    what's the most wonderful, amazing thing that could
    happen if you spoke to someone about Jesus?
4. If you were raised in a Christian home, was evangelism
    part of your family culture? If yes, how so?
5. Do you know the names of your neighbors? Do you know
    them well enough to know the brokenness or blessings
    of their lives?
6. In what areas in your life are you not passionately pursu-
    ing a life that glorifies God?
7. What is one thing you could do today to overcome an
    obstacle to glorifying God in that area of life?

8.   Reflect on this statement: "If you feel as if you should share Jesus with someone, it's probably not the world, your flesh, or the devil prompting you to do it. Take the risk."

9.   Think about someone you know who doesn't know Jesus. Write down that person's name. Pray for him or her. (You don't have to witness to them this week, but it's okay if you do!)

10. *Who's Your One?* In the blank below, write the name of one person, *your one*, and commit to the Lord that you will seek to influence this person for Christ each week over the next eight weeks.

MY ONE IS . . . _____

Topics for Prayer

1.   Pray for help to face and overcome your fears about life-style evangelism.

2.   Pray for help to meet your neighbors—if you haven't already—and for relationships with them.

3.   Pray for opportunities to share Jesus with someone, somewhere, in some way.

> *God, I know you love people. Give me an opportunity today to help someone see your love for them and hear how they can enjoy your work in Jesus Christ. Give me the boldness to talk with them about Jesus.*

Week 2

*Principle #2: You don't have to prove the claims
of Christianity, just present them clearly.*

Scriptures for Meditation

"I passed on to you as most important what I also received:
that Christ died for our sins according to the Scriptures, that
he was buried, that he was raised on the third day according
to the Scriptures, and that he appeared to Cephas, then to the
Twelve." (1 Cor 15:3–5)

"My soul, bless the LORD, and all that is within me, bless his
holy name. My soul, bless the LORD, and do not forget all his
benefits. He forgives all your iniquity; he heals all your dis-
eases. He redeems your life from the Pit; he crowns you with
faithful love and compassion. He satisfies you with good things;
your youth is renewed like the eagle." (Ps 103:1–5)

Questions for Reflection and Application

1. Have you ever thought of yourself as an evangelist?
2. Think back over something positive from your life that
   you've shared on social media, or with friends or family
   members in person. Was it stressful to share that exciting
   event, or was it natural and fun?
3. Look again at the story of the gospel. What are the four
   major points of its plotline? Can you see how they relate
   to plotlines in movies, novels, or other stories?
4. Think about a favorite movie or story. Why do you love
   it so much? How does it move you? How does your favorite movie or story reflect something of the message of
   Scripture?

5. How can you connect the themes or plotline of your favorite movie or story to the redemptive plot of Scripture? Jot down several connection points and practice talking through these with yourself this week, in preparation for sharing them with others.

6. How have you experienced God's benefits? Look at Psalm 103. See how David reflects on God's *Forgiveness, Greatness, Healing, Blessing, Satisfaction,* and *Faithfulness.* Take time each day this week to think about the many benefits the Lord has given you.

7. *Who's Your One?* This week, think of at least one way the plotline of Scripture might connect with *your one.*

Topics for Prayer

1. For God to continue helping you grow in your understanding of the wonder of his gospel.

2. For God to grow in you a desire to share Christ with those around you.

3. For God to help you love those around you with his love.

> *God, I know you love people. Give me an opportunity today to help someone see your love for them and hear how they can enjoy your work in Jesus Christ. Give me the boldness to talk with them about Jesus.*

Week 3

Principle #3: Gospel conversations are better for everyone.

Scriptures for Meditation

"Paul stood in the middle of the Areopagus and said: 'People of Athens! I see that you are extremely religious in every respect. For as I was passing through and observing the objects of your worship, I even found an altar on which was inscribed: "To an Unknown God." Therefore, what you worship in ignorance, this I proclaim to you. The God who made the world and everything in it—he is Lord of heaven and earth—does not live in shrines made by hands. Neither is he served by human hands, as though he needed anything, since he himself gives everyone life and breath and all things.'" (Acts 17:22–25)

"Act wisely toward outsiders, making the most of the time. Let your speech always be gracious, seasoned with salt, so that you may know how you should answer each person." (Col 4:5–6)

Questions for Reflection and Application

1. Is there somewhere you like to meet people for conversations? Coffee shop? Restaurant? Break room? Park? Lake? Or do you enjoy talking with others during an activity such as fishing, hunting, gardening, or playing games?
2. Have you ever introduced to each other two people you care about? Did you hope they would date? Become friends? Learn something from each other? How did the introductions make you feel? Were you nervous or uncomfortable, did you enjoy it?
3. What are three things people can tell about us from our conversations? Pay attention to your conversations

this week and see what you can learn about the people you are talking with. Do they care about you? How can you tell if they believe what they are talking about?

4.   Now consider this: What do your interactions and conversations say to others about whether you really care for them?

5.   Over the next week, pay special attention to the things people say in your presence and what they post on their social media accounts. How often do others mention things that cause them pain or bring them pleasure? See if you can identify what others are hopeful for, afraid of, hurting from, or dreaming about. Keep a running list of examples and consider how the gospel might speak to those areas of life.

6.   At least one time this week, try to connect the gospel to a specific situation in the life of someone else.

7.   How many opportunities can you identify this week to share Jesus through everyday conversation with others?

8.   *Who's Your One?* Make time this week to have a conversation with *your one.*

Topics for Prayer

1.   For God to give you clear opportunities to connect with others through everyday conversations.

2.   For God to help you continue to develop as an evangelist.

3.   For God to guide you to connect on a spiritual level with at least one unbeliever (at work, at school, in your family, or in your neighborhood) with whom you share a long-term relationship.

> *God, I know you love people. Give me an opportunity today to help someone see your love for them and hear how they can enjoy your work in Jesus Christ. Give me the boldness to talk with them about Jesus.*

Week 4

Principle #4: Every context is an opportunity to
share the joy of the gospel with others.

Scriptures for Meditation

"From one man [God] has made every nationality to live over the whole earth and has determined their appointed times and the boundaries of where they live." (Acts 17:26)

"You are a chosen race, a royal priesthood, a holy nation, a people for his possession, so that you may proclaim the praises of the one who called you out of darkness into his marvelous light. Once you were not a people, but now you are God's people; you had not received mercy, but now you have received mercy." (1 Pet 2:9–10)

Questions for Reflection and Application

1. God did not make a mistake in how he made you or where he placed you in the world. Take some time to think about the ways you are unique. Write down at least three or four specific ways that God has wired you for his glory. Thank him for how he has made you.

2. Your location, your position in life, and your current situation form a platform for the gospel. Jot down at least two ways you think your current situation can provide you with opportunities to share Christ.

3. What personal limitation in your life would you change if you could?

4. Read this Bible verse: "But he said to me, 'My grace is sufficient for you, for my power is perfected in weakness.' Therefore, I will most gladly boast all the more about my weaknesses, so that Christ's power may reside in me. So I

take pleasure in weaknesses, insults, hardships, persecutions, and in difficulties, for the sake of Christ. For when I am weak, then I am strong" (2 Cor 12:9–10). How can God use your limitation for his glory? Can you relate better to certain people because of it? Is your faith stronger as a result of it?

5.   Which things in your life deepen your affection for Jesus? What diminishes your love for him? What is one thing you can begin doing and one thing you can stop doing so that your love for Jesus will grow?

6.   How is sharing Christ different from selling a product?

7.   *Who's Your One?* This week, think of ways you can bring joy to others. Also, do something this week to serve *your one* and help that person experience the joy of Jesus.

Topics for Prayer

1.   For God to help you grow in your ability to share Jesus.

2.   Pray by name for the people in your different circles of concern who do not know Jesus. If you know only believers, ask God to help you establish a relationship with at least one unbeliever.

3.   For God to give you the courage and creativity to bring gospel joy to others.

4.   For God to provide opportunity to bring joy to *your one* this week.

> *God, I know you love people. Give me an opportunity today to help someone see your love for them and hear how they can enjoy your work in Jesus Christ. Give me the boldness to talk with them about Jesus.*

Week 5

*Principle #5: The issues people face are open
doors to connect the gospel to them.*

Scriptures for Meditation

"I give you a new command: Love one another. Just as I have loved you, you are also to love one another. By this everyone will know that you are my disciples, if you love one another." (John 13:34–35)

"I pray that your participation in the faith may become effective through knowing every good thing that is in us for the glory of Christ. For I have great joy and encouragement from your love, because the hearts of the saints have been refreshed through you, brother." (Phlm 1:6–7)

Questions for Reflection and Application

1. Let's take some time to evaluate and improve our prayer lives:
    a. How are you praying that God will help you live out the gospel?
    b. How are you praying that God will help you further develop your ability to witness for him?
    c. Who are you praying for daily? Are you asking God to give you an opportunity to share Jesus with someone? Who? Are you praying daily for *your one*?
    d. What fears and insecurities are you praying that God will take away—or use for his glory?
    e. How has your prayer life improved over the past month?

  f. Take a few minutes to thank God for the growth you have experienced in the past several weeks. Ask him to help you continue to mature in Christ.

2. Which of the five keys for healthy conversation seem most natural for you?

3. Can you think of one person with whom you can talk this week and apply this key during the conversation?

4. Sometime this week, try to use one of the other conversation keys as an opportunity for sharing Jesus. Take a few minutes to reflect on this experience. What went well? How could you improve?

5. Consider beginning, or maintaining, a prayer journal that records your requests as well as God's answers to your prayers.

6. *Who's Your One?* Pray every day this week for *your one* and ask God to give you an opportunity to talk with that person. Be alert for the thought of Jesus to come to mind. If it does, try to introduce him into the conversation.

Topics for Prayer

1. For God to help you live the gospel well.

2. For God to continue to give you a gospel love for others.

3. For God to provide you with an opportunity to show Christian love for at least one nonbeliever whose lifestyle or life choices you do not endorse. Look past their actions and try to minister to that person. Are they hurting and needing encouragement? Do they feel unnoticed and unloved, and could they use a reminder that they are seen and cared about?

> *God, I know you love people. Give me an opportunity today to help someone see your love for them and hear how they can enjoy your work in Jesus Christ. Give me the boldness to talk with them about Jesus.*

Week 6

Principle #6: People are already interested in what is best for them; the gospel is best for all people.

Scriptures for Meditation

"Jesus said, 'Everyone who drinks from this water will get thirsty again. But whoever drinks from the water that I will give him will never get thirsty again. In fact, the water I will give him will become a well of water springing up in him for eternal life.'" (John 4:13–14)

"For God loved the world in this way: He gave his one and only Son, so that everyone who believes in him will not perish but have eternal life. For God did not send his Son into the world to condemn the world, but to save the world through him." (John 3:16–17)

Questions for Reflection and Application

1. Ask a friend, coworker, neighbor, or family member to tell you the story of their life. You can ask about how they grew up, how they met their spouse, or how they got "here." If you already know most of these stories about the person, see if there is an area of their life where you can catch up. What parts of the story can you empathize with? Are there parts of their story that you identify with? How might you retell their story in a way that includes Jesus and his ability to change lives?
2. Think about a sphere of life that you care about (sports, politics, art, economics, education, etc.). As you talk with

others about this interest, pay attention to the ways you might relate the gospel to this topic.

3. Do you really expect others to believe that the gospel is good news? Take some time to think about why you perhaps struggle to believe this biblical truth.

4. How has your understanding of evangelism changed as a result of this study? How much of your evangelism is about loving and serving, and how much is about performance and presentation? Explain your answer.

5. What great things are you expecting God to do within your relational circles? How are you praying for your neighborhood, school, place of work?

6. In what ways can you empathize with the pain and pleasure, the fears and hopes, of others? How has Christ rewritten the story of your life? In what ways can you relate this to others?

7. Think about the last conversation you had with an unbeliever. To what extent did you show love, kindness, and gentleness, and to what extent did you find yourself judging him or her because of their lifestyle, appearance, language, or habits?

8. *Who's Your One?* What do you know about the life story of *your one?* Have you shared with him or her how Jesus transformed your life?

Topics for Prayer

1. For an expectation that those around you will be open to hearing the gospel and will receive it as good news.

2. For God to do something amazing in your social sphere.

3. For God to help you identify with someone this week and engage with that person in their exact moment of need.

4. For God to give you a growing discernment to help you confidently identify others' areas of pain, pleasure, hope, and fear.

   God, I know you love people. Give me an opportunity today to help someone see your love for them and hear how they can enjoy your work in Jesus Christ. Give me the boldness to talk with them about Jesus.

Week 7

*Principle #7: Gospel conversations must be grounded
in relationships, both with Jesus and with others.*

Scriptures for Meditation

"In your hearts regard Christ the Lord as holy, ready at any
time to give a defense to anyone who asks you for a reason for
the hope that is in you. Yet do this with gentleness and respect,
keeping a clear conscience, so that when you are accused,
those who disparage your good conduct in Christ will be put to
shame." (1 Pet 3:15–16)

"The fruit of the Spirit is love, joy, peace, patience, kindness,
goodness, faithfulness, gentleness, and self-control. The law is
not against such things. Now those who belong to Christ Jesus
have crucified the flesh with its passions and desires. If we live
by the Spirit, let us also keep in step with the Spirit. Let us
not become conceited, provoking one another, envying one
another." (Gal 5:22–26)

Questions for Reflection and Application

1. What is the first image that comes to mind when you
    think about evangelism? Is it something that happens
    with a stranger or a friend? Can you imagine sharing
    Christ with someone in your family?
2. What are two questions about the gospel or the Bible you
    don't know the answer to and are afraid someone will
    ask? Spend some time this week researching answers.
    Think about how you can explain your answers to a
    nonbeliever.

3. Think of three people you observed living in such a way that you could say you saw Jesus through them. Write out what they did that made Jesus more real to you.

4. Reflect on this statement: "The closer you are to someone, the less your words matter and the more your actions matter." Think about those closest to you. How can you live so that your words about Jesus are validated?

5. Look at the list you made from your concentric circles. Who on the list are you most concerned about? Who do you think is the closest to trusting Jesus? Who is furthest away? If you think of the principle of "plus one," what is that person's next step toward Jesus?

6. *Who's Your One?* What is his or her next step toward trusting Jesus? How can you adjust your life to help that person see the gospel or hear the gospel verbally from you?

Topics for Prayer

1. For God to help you establish a witnessing rhythm that is right for your context.

2. For the Holy Spirit to guide you to show the gospel with your life as well as to share it with your lips.

3. For God to deepen your willingness to pay the price and bear the burden of living an evangelistic lifestyle.

> *God, I know you love people. Give me an opportunity today to help someone see your love for them and hear how they can enjoy your work in Jesus Christ. Give me the boldness to talk with them about Jesus.*

Week 8

*Principle #8: A Jesus-sharing lifestyle starts with a
plan to share Jesus as a part of everyday living.*

Scriptures for Meditation

"'Follow me,' [Jesus] told them, 'and I will make you fish for
people.' Immediately [Simon and Andrew] left their nets and
followed him." (Matt 4:19–20)

"You will receive power when the Holy Spirit has come on you,
and you will be my witnesses in Jerusalem, in all Judea and
Samaria, and to the end of the earth." (Acts 1:8)

"Jesus came near and said to them, 'All authority has been
given to me in heaven and on earth. Go, therefore, and make
disciples of all nations, baptizing them in the name of the
Father and of the Son and of the Holy Spirit, teaching them
to observe everything I have commanded you. And remember,
I am with you always, to the end of the age.'" (Matt 28:18–20)

Questions for Reflection and Application

1. In what ways is your life gospel-focused?
2. What do you understand about your specific giftedness,
   calling, and opportunities? What has God made you good
   at? What are you passionate about? What unique opportunities has God given you (think: people, places, situations)?
3. Write out some ways you can share Jesus out of the sweet
   spot of your life.
4. Consider the steps for living an evangelistic life. Which
   of these are most challenging for you?

5. What plans do you have for developing an evangelistic lifestyle? Are you ready to commit to the life we have called you to? Why or why not?

6. Review your notes from the past eight weeks. What has God shown you—people, principles, opportunities— that you are most thankful for? What have you made part of your life that you hope you never forget?

7. How can you make evangelism part of your family culture?

8. Write one or two paragraphs describing your plan for sharing Christ regularly.

9. *Who's Your One?* How has God used you to influence *your one* for Christ? What are the next steps you believe you need to take?

Topics for Prayer

1. For God to prepare you and use you in the lives of others.

2. For God to anchor the principles of this book in your mind so that you will not forget all that he has taught you.

3. For God to continue to help you grow as a witness, giving you eyes to see opportunities and the boldness to step out in faith—to share Jesus without freaking out.

> *God, I know you love people. Give me an opportunity today to help someone see your love for them and hear how they can enjoy your work in Jesus Christ. Give me the boldness to talk with them about Jesus.*

Study Questions for Small Groups

These questions are designed to help you personalize the information provided in this book. They can be used for classroom discussion, church small groups, book clubs, or even among a group of friends.

Work through each question and encourage each member to contribute to the group. Allow the discussion to be part of the learning experience.

Close each session in prayer. Pray for one another and for evangelistic opportunities.

Chapter 1

1. What about sharing the gospel most freaks you out? Share these concerns with your group.
2. How comfortable are you when it comes to retelling the story of the gospel according to Scripture?
3. Do you currently have authentic relationships with non-Christians? If so, think of ways you have already both shown and shared the gospel in those relationships. If not, begin to pray that God would show you how your life is and can be intersecting naturally with those who need the good news.
4. If you have shared the gospel with others before, what about your approach or method do you want to change or adjust after reading this chapter?

5. Assuming you are a Christian, does your life reflect God's work and a message that would accurately explain what that work is? Why or why not? What steps do you need to take to share the gospel more accurately with your life and lips?

Chapter 2

1. When reading the Old Testament, what are some ways you find that it describes and explains the life, death, and resurrection of Jesus?
2. In this chapter, you learned that the Bible is one story that follows a four-part story line: Creation, Provision, Fall, and Promise. In your group, break up into pairs and practice sharing a summary of each part of the story line and why it is essential. Don't get discouraged if you can't remember everything; the goal is not to repeat it word-for-word. The more you practice, the easier it will become.
3. Use the "Sharing the Story of the Gospel" Appendix to help you learn the gospel. Pay close attention to details that you may be leaving out or adding when sharing the story. Find ways to develop a personal gospel fluency and discuss them with the group.
4. Is Jesus the central figure in the story of your life, or is he merely a tangential character who appears only infrequently, perhaps just on Sundays? What are some ways you can adjust your life so that Jesus is the acknowledged hero of your story? Discuss ways in which each of you can step out of your own story and enter into God's.

Chapter 3

1. Imagine what it would look like for you, over coffee with a friend, to talk about God's work in your life. Would it

seem easy or difficult? What does the answer to this question say about your relationship with God?

2. Do you think you could incorporate into your everyday conversations discussion about your walk with Jesus? Why or why not?

3. Look again at the differences between a gospel presentation and a gospel conversation. Discuss why a person is much more likely to gain an understanding of the gospel through a relationship with a Christian than through a presentation given by a stranger.

4. Prayer is a spiritual discipline that is essential for any Christian who desires to share Jesus with others. Discuss three ways prayer helps Christians with evangelism. Do you practice a regular habit of prayer?

5. Why do you think people find it difficult to relax when they talk about their relationship with Jesus?

Chapter 4

1. Do you find yourself more comfortable using methods of evangelism or casually communicating Christ through an ordinary life of gospel storytelling? What habits and practices in your life help you communicate the gospel story without freaking out?

2. As you read 1 Pet 2:9–12, discuss what those statements say is true about you as a believer. How do these identifiers point to God's gracious work in your life?

3. Discuss practical ways in which your good works demonstrate God's grace in your life. Does your lifestyle show your personal belief in the story of the gospel? Does it validate the claims you make of Christ?

4. How can you better embrace who God made you to be in order to establish authentic relationships with other people? Discuss how you can use the various contexts of your life to make much of the grace of God in Christ.

Chapter 5

1. When it comes to sharing Jesus with others, do you suffer from analysis paralysis? Do you find it difficult just to get started? Do you overthink the process and create unnecessary pressure for yourself? Discuss with your group how knowing that the Holy Spirit lives powerfully within you can move you beyond your insecurities to talk about Jesus.

2. Would you consider yourself a person of prayer? Why or why not? From the chapter, discuss the four things you should pray each day and how they are essential for becoming a faithful evangelist.

3. As a group, recap the five keys to healthy conversations that help Christians engage in gospel conversations in an era that is so influenced by social media and technology. Get into pairs and practice some of the spiritual questions that have been provided to transition the conversation, as well as those that follow the biblical narrative. This will help you become more comfortable using them in conversation.

4. To share Jesus without freaking out, what changes and/ or steps do you need to take to better enter into life-changing conversations and relationships with others?

Chapter 6

1. Look over the different spheres and the examples mentioned in this chapter for engaging others with biblical truths. Discuss as a group how you can leverage them for sharing Jesus.

2. Begin to train yourself to hear God's story in others' stories. Discuss with your group the three pieces of advice in this chapter for transitioning from someone's story to the gospel story. What stands out to you, and why? Share

with one another some ways you can begin to use this advice in your current relationships with non-Christians.

3. Share with the group some of the other contexts that currently describe your life. What are the areas of brokenness and blessing that can be observed? How can you share the gospel there?

4. How did the discussion about "plus one" in this chapter make you feel about your responsibility for another person's salvation? Were you encouraged, or did it increase the pressure for whether or not a person decides to trust in Jesus as their personal Savior? Does this give you confidence and freedom in your evangelism? Discuss with your group ways in which you can help your non-Christian friends move one step closer toward a saving knowledge of Jesus.

Chapter 7

1. Do you have relationships with non-Christians? Do you struggle with relating to and/or sharing Jesus with people who are not like you? Take time now to go through the exercise on pages 103–5 to identify different relationships you have and the current spiritual state of those people.

2. Since reading this book, have you been praying for opportunities to share your faith? Has God put seekers in your path? Discuss with your group whether or not the three questions given in this chapter were helpful in discerning divine appointments. Share a conversation you may have had about Jesus and whether or not you were able to share without freaking out.

3. Do you have family members or close friends who are non-Christians? If so, does sharing Jesus with those closest to you make you uncomfortable? Think about your

life and identify things that could hinder those closest to you from seeing a changed life. Pray and ask God to help you make your life speak more clearly of his saving grace.

4. Experience proves that the longer we wait to share Christ in a new relationship, the less likely we are ever to do it. Have you already found this to be true in your relationships? Discuss ways you can be more intentional in sharing Christ earlier in a relationship without being obnoxious or freaking out.

5. Discuss with your group the four helpful points to any objection that may come your way when sharing Jesus. Have you ever experienced hostility when sharing? If so, think about that conversation and discuss together how the four points mentioned in this chapter could have been helpful. If not, share something you will take away from these points to help you in future conversations.

Chapter 8

1. Go back to the "Sharing the Story of the Gospel" appendix and review the gospel story. Break up in pairs and take turns retelling the story of the gospel to one another. Take turns sharing your stories (your testimonies) as well.

2. With your group, go through the steps to an evangelistic life and discuss what stood out to you and why. Also, share what seems difficult, and which action steps you plan to take to make your conversations about Christ more enjoyable for both you and others.

3. Talk with your group about your answers regarding your *Giftedness, Calling,* and *Opportunities.* Were you able to identify ways to share Jesus?